HANDEL'S
Will

FACSIMILES
AND COMMENTARY

EDITED BY DONALD BURROWS

THE GERALD COKE HANDEL FOUNDATION

First published 2009 by
The Gerald Coke Handel Foundation
40 Brunswick Square
London WC1N 1AZ

© 2008 The Gerald Coke Handel Foundation

British Library Cataloguing-in-Publication Data
A Catalogue record for this book is available
from The British Library

ISBN 978 0 9560 9980 8 (hardback)
ISBN 978 0 9560 9981 5 (paperback)

Designed in Baskerville by Geoff Green Book Design, Cambridge
Printed and bound by Henry Ling Ltd, Dorchester

Illustrations from the Gerald Coke Handel Collection

The facsimiles on pp. 61 and 62 are slightly reduced

The Gerald Coke Handel Foundation, founded by Gerald Coke's family and
named after him, promotes education and research in eighteenth-century
music, particularly relating to the life and works of George Frideric
Handel, by supporting the Gerald Coke Handel Collection
at the Foundling Museum.

CONTENTS

Introduction DONALD BURROWS	5
Handel and his will ELLEN T. HARRIS	9
Handel's German relatives KLAUS-PETER KOCH	21
An exceptional estate RICHARD CREWDSON	25
Translations of French texts TERENCE BEST	30
Transcription of German text KLAUS-PETER KOCH	31
Specifications of the documents	32
FACSIMILES	
The Coke Copy	35
The Probate Copy	45
The Executor's Copy (extracts)	59

INTRODUCTION

DONALD BURROWS

THE MANUSCRIPT will of George Frideric Handel, written on 1 June 1750, with the accompanying codicils signed by the composer in 1756, 1757 and 1759, is one of the most important items in the Gerald Coke Handel Collection (now established at the Foundling Museum in Brunswick Square, London). It forms a fitting complement to the rich thematic collection – including early manuscript and printed scores, word-books of operas and oratorios, and portraits of relevant musicians – that Gerald Coke (1907-1990) had assembled over a period of about 60 years during the twentieth century.[1] Mr Coke's purchase of the will from an American owner was negotiated by the book-dealer Percy Muir during the 1930s, and for security reasons it was not kept with the rest of his Handel collection during the Second World War: for part of that time it resided instead in Mrs Coke's handbag.[2] Previously the will had been owned by the singer, scholar and collector William H. Cummings (1831-1915), and it appears in the sale catalogue of his collection in 1917. While in his ownership, a transcript of the will's text, with facsimiles of Handel's signatures, was published in the 'Handel number' of *The Musical Times* in December 1893, and again in Cummings's subsequent short biography of Handel.[3] At the Cummings sale the will was purchased by the book-dealer Maggs Brothers Ltd for £210, and it passed briefly to another owner: it appeared again in the sale of the property of Parke Mayhew Pittar in 1918, when it was purchased by 'Moreton' (probably another dealer) for £270.[4] Following Handel's death in 1759 the will was used by his London executor George Amyand (1720-66) for the administration of the bequests, and after Amyand's death it probably remained the property of his family. It was subsequently owned by William Snoxell (c. 1797-1879), and Cummings purchased it for £53 at the sale of Snoxell's property in 1879.[5] Snoxell had owned the will by 1857, when it was referred to in Victor Schoelcher's biography of Handel.[6]

To mark the 250th anniversary of Handel's death in 1759, the Gerald Coke Handel Foundation presents this facsimile publication of Handel's will, along with some essays that provide commentary on, and context for, this remarkable document. The facsimile of the document from the Coke Collection is accompanied by facsimiles of other relevant contemporary material.

As leaseholder of his house in Brook Street, Handel owned no real estate, so the will and codicils relate entirely to personalty. The original will thus did not require the extra formalities of witnesses that would have been needed for the dispositions of land and houses.[7] Indeed, under the relevant act of 1705 the holograph will did not even need to be signed, though Handel did so. However, by the time Handel came to add the codicils he was not able to write out the document on account of his blindness, nor presumably to read the text, so two witnesses were necessary in each case to attest to the fact that the testator had had the codicil read to him before he signed it. John Hetherington and Thomas Harris, who had been witnesses to previous codicils, were named as beneficiaries in the last codicil, and hence were not eligible as witnesses on that occasion.

The 1750 will is obviously a very personal document, and we do not know how much professional advice, if any, Handel sought before drafting it. No doubt he used at least one other English will as a model, and if indeed he had studied law at Halle University in his youth he may have felt competent to avoid ambiguities in the

---

1 On the history of the Collection, see Gerald Coke, 'Collecting Handel', in Terence Best (ed.), *Handel Collections and their History* (Oxford, 1993), pp. 1-9.

2 Gerald Coke owned the will by May 1937, when it was the subject of a valuation (£1,000). Percival Horace Muir (1894-1979) was a partner in the book-dealers Elkin Mathews.

3 *Catalogue of the Famous Musical Library of Books, Manuscripts, Autograph Letters[,] Musical Scores, etc. The Property of the late W. H. Cummings, Mus. Doc,* (Sotheby, Wilkinson and Hodge, London; 17, 18 and 21-24 May 1917), First Day, Lot 135; *The Musical Times and Singing-class Circular*, 14 December 1893, pp. 20-21; William H. Cummings, *Handel* (London, 1904), pp. 66-72.

4 *Catalogue of Valuable Books and Manuscripts, being the second and concluding portion of the library of the late P. M. Pittar of 14, Cleveland Square, Hyde Park, W.* (Sotheby, Wilkinson and Hodge, London; 4-7 November 1918), Second Day, Lot 304.

5 *Catalogue of Autographs and Manuscripts of the late William Snoxell esq. ... including ... the original autograph will with codicils of George Frideric Handel* (Puttick and Simpson; London, 21 July 1879), Lot 80. The sale also included the inventory of Handel's household goods (now British Library Egerton MS 3009, ff. 17-18) which had presumably also been Amyand's property: see Otto Erich Deutsch, *Handel: A Documentary Biography* (London, 1955), pp. 829-31.

6 Victor Schoelcher, *The Life of Handel* (1857), p. 344, following a transcription of the will text from the Probate Copy (pp. 340-4); also a footnote on p. 325 ('The duplicate copy is in the possession of an amateur, Mr. Snoxell, who holds it from the heir of Amyant, Handel's testamentary executor') which was probably the source for a similar statement in W. S. Rockstro, *The Life of George Frederick Handel* (London, 1883), p. 369, where Snoxell is identified as 'of Charterhouse Square'; see also W. H. Cummings, 'A Few Words about Handel', *Proceedings of the Musical Association*, vi (1880-1), p. 31. Amyand's immediate heir was presumably George Cornewall (1748-1819), whose sister married James Harris (the son of Handel's friend and supporter of the same name) in 1778.

7 The legal requirement for witnesses to wills involving personalty was introduced by the Wills Act of 1837.

expression of his intentions. The wording is a little archaic, especially in the repeated use of the word 'Item'. After the initial bequests to his servant, professional associate and his friend James Hunter, the will deals exclusively with the disposal of his substantial investment income: he was in fact following the usual convention by distributing the estate among his relatives.[8] However, these legatees were physically distant and also relatively distant in terms of family relationship: a considerable international correspondence must have taken place during the 1750s, reporting on changes in the family and establishing the present whereabouts of his continental relatives.[9] If Handel had sought professional legal advice in 1750, he would have been dissuaded from appointing his niece in Saxony as Sole Executrix, as any lawyer would have seen at once the potential inconvenience and risk to the assets of the estate during the weeks that would elapse between the date of death and the conveyance of news to the niece, following which she would either have to travel to London or appoint an Attorney with full power to deal with the administration. It comes as no surprise that one of the provisions of the first codicil is the appointment of an English co-executor. Handel's principal adviser for the drafting of the codicils was probably Thomas Harris, a London lawyer from a family in his social circle and the recipient (during Handel's lifetime, and thus not as a bequest) of the famous 'Malmesbury' portrait of the composer by Philip Mercier.

George Amyand took the Executor's Oath before the Surrogate (the officer who acted with the authority of the Chancellor of the Consistory Court) on the very day of Handel's death, thereby assuming immediate full responsibility for, and control over, the assets of the estate. There was nothing thereafter to delay the commencement of the Executorship, as there was no tax to pay: death duties were not introduced until 1796. When Amyand took the oath it was noted that power was reserved for Johanna Floercke, the co-executor, to participate in the Administration. There is no definite evidence that she exercised this power directly in London, but she was probably responsible for the distribution to the German relatives from the overall sum transferred from London by Amyand. The business of the legacies to the Taust family and the protested Bill of Exchange, which is the subject of one of the documents reproduced in this facsimile, is an interesting one from the legal point of view, because it raises the question of whether, as English law stood, the death of the fifth child in the family during Handel's lifetime meant that the legacy to him or her automatically lapsed, or passed to his or her heirs, and whether in this case the matter should be decided according to English or local German law. There is an ambiguity in the wording of the relevant codicil, but the Executor was probably correct under English law in declaring that the legacy had lapsed: the dispute could have gone to court, but the relatives in Halle probably decided that the expense was not worthwhile.

'Handel's will' is not a simple document existing in a single copy, but is represented by at least four related and authoritative copies. Some aspects of the relationships between, and purposes of, the various copies are uncertain, and for this publication I have adopted terms to distinguish them that are entirely unofficial but reflect their provenance. The 'Coke Copy' is matched by an almost identical copy (the 'Probate Copy') now in The [British] National Archives at Kew, from the archives of the Prerogative Court of Canterbury (reference PROB 1/14). In both copies the original will is written entirely by Handel; the supplementary codicils added at later dates are written by other people, but they are signed by Handel and by witnesses to his signature. A couple of drafting corrections to the original will in the Coke Copy are incorporated into the text of the other copy, establishing a probable sequence.[10] Most likely, the will and codicils in PROB 1/14 were the legal copy deposited with the Court after Handel's death in order to initiate the Probate procedure so that the terms of the will could be executed, while the Coke Copy was Handel's personal copy, which was made available immediately after his death to Amyand as his London executor. According to an affidavit that is now also found in PROB 1/14, the will and codicils were 'found locked and sealed

---

[8] There was overall consistency in the value of that part of Handel's estate that he designated for his German relatives, through the various stages of the will and its codicils: see Ellen T. Harris, 'Handel the Investor', *Music & Letters*, 85/4 (2004), pp. 521–75, esp. pp. 555–6. An accumulation of wealth enabled him to make substantial bequests elsewhere in the final codicil.

[9] It is possible that Handel's bequest to the 'Secretary for the affairs of Hanover' in the final codicil of the will was in recognition of assistance over communications between London and his relatives abroad. In a letter of 22 June 1750 to Johann Gottfried Taust, Handel mentioned that he had recently made his will: see Hans Joachim Marx, 'Ein unveröffentlichter Brief Händels in Harvard', in Hans Joachim Marx (ed.), *Göttinger Händel-Beiträge*, ii (1986), pp. 221–5.

[10] The Coke Copy, as probably the earliest surviving version, might perhaps be regarded as the 'original' from which the others are copies. It seems more appropriate, however, to treat all the parallel documents as copies of the same text, since the priority is not certain; the situation is further confused by Handel's own use of 'original'. In spite of some small revisions, the Coke Copy is so tidily written as to suggest that it was itself a fair copy from an earlier draft.

up together in a Cover in the said dec[eas]ed's bureau in his ... Dwelling House in Brook Street', and we would expect the accompanying copy to have been the one that was referred to.[11] However, an endorsement in Handel's hand on a page (reproduced in this facsimile) that was formerly attached to the Coke Copy says that 'The Original of this is deposited in the hands of Messieurs Voguel and Amyand Marchands of London', suggesting that Handel kept the Coke Copy and deposited PROB 1/14 with Amyand, but it was the latter copy (rather than the one found in Handel's bureau - i.e. the Coke Copy) that was submitted for probate. Handel's reference to PROB 1/14 as the 'Original' (in the sense of the earlier copy) seems to conflict with the facts: perhaps he was intending to indicate that that copy was to be taken as the primary legal document. Amyand presumably took the copy that Handel had deposited with him when he registered as executor, leaving it with the Court and subsequently taking charge of the copy found in Handel's bureau, so that in effect an exchange took place. The existence of two copies would have assured a certain security, particularly if Handel deposited them in different places, but if disputes were to be avoided it was necessary to ensure that the texts remained identical: for this reason, the deletion of the bequest to James Hunter had to be repeated in both copies. The style of the handwriting in Handel's annotation suggests that it was written in 1751 or 1752: perhaps he decided that it was prudent to put a copy into some form of safe custody when he became aware that his blindness was advancing. This would have been about five years before he named Amyand as co-executor, but it looks as if the process that led to the first codicil had already begun.

An empty leaf attached to the original will in the Probate Copy was used to record the landmarks in the probate process: confirmation of the testator's death, confirmation of the validity of the will, and the 'proving' of the will twelve days later. The Probate Copy is accompanied by two sworn affidavits: one from William Brinck and Edward Cavendish, confirming Handel's handwriting in the will, and one from John Duburk, Handel's servant, confirming that the will as produced for the court was indeed the composer's final form of the document, including the deletion of a phrase in the bequest to Hunter.

The text of the will, the codicils, the affidavits, and the endorsement marking the completion of the probate procedure, was copied in a formal handwriting by a scribe into one of the Court's ledger books (the 'Ledger Copy', The National Archives PROB/11/845, ff. 268v-270v). Yet another copy of the will and codicils, with a signed declaration of the probate, was made, apparently for the German co-executor (now Royal College of Music, London, MS 2190), the 'Executor's Copy'. This is accompanied by further copies of extracts from the will and codicils, also apparently made for the German relatives (MS 2191), and copies of legal documents, in French, relating to the legal challenge by the Taust family to Amyand's administration of their bequest (MS 2192). Documents in the archives of the Bank of England record Amyand's activity in disbursing the contents of Handel's stock accounts in accordance with Handel's bequests, once he had registered his right to do so under the Probate, but these do not involve any copies of extracts from the will itself.[12]

The facsimile reproduces all pages of the two primary documents for the will and its codicils, the Coke Copy (with the additional leaf that has now become separated) and the Probate Copy, but the empty pages with the affidavits that accompany the Probate Copy are not included. The Ledger Copy (not reproduced here) adds nothing new to the text, and the same can be said of the text of the will as it is found in the Executor's Copy. However, the pages of the latter copy which have annotations or signatures (MS 2190 f. 1r, f. 3v) are included. The material in MS 2191 is also basically repetitive of the text as found elsewhere:

f. 1r: Copy of the third codicil

ff. 1v-2r: Copies of the fourth codicil and the Probate statement

Seal on the Coke copy of Handel's will

11 Seal-impressions on red wax, perhaps as confirmation of the authenticity of the document, are found on the fourth codicil in the Coke Copy (f. 4v) and the Probate Copy (f. 5v). Both of the copies were probably also enclosed in envelopes or wrappers on which the loose ends of paper were secured with a similar application of wax; to have the will was thus 'sealed up' provided security against interference, until the contents were opened by breaking the seal.

12 Transcripts of the relevant Memorandum and of the closing account were first published in Percy M. Young, *Handel* (London, 1947), and are printed in Deutsch, *Handel*, pp. 821, 838. On the subject of the bequests and their monetary value, see Harris, 'Handel the Investor', pp. 552-7.

f. 2v: Copy of clauses from the will and first codicil, relating to bequests to the Taust family.

The copies of the codicils were probably taken directly from MS 2190. The text on f. 1r is translated into German, written in *Kurrentschrift*, and the other pages have defects of transcription which indicate that the scribe was not an English speaker. The paper is of a different type from MSS 2190 and 2192, and it seems probable that MS 2191 was copied in Germany.[13] In this facsimile only two pages from MS 2191 are included: the page in *Kurrentschrift* (f. 1r), and the page with an annotation (f. 2v). Both sides of the first leaf of MS 2192 are reproduced, but not the blank leaf to which it is attached.

In general, the English texts in the documents are written clearly enough to be understood by the modern reader. Translations of the French annotations and texts from MSS 2190 and 2192 are given on p. 30, followed by a literal transcription of the *Kurrentschrift* text from MS 2191.

The essays that follow this introduction have been gathered in order to provide commentaries on some aspects of the will. Ellen Harris deals with the content of the will itself, in the context of Handel's life and social relationships during his last decade; Klaus-Peter Koch elucidates the family structure that encompassed the various relatives that are named in the will; and Richard Crewdson compares Handel's will (and estate) with the fortunes of some other prominent eighteenth-century musicians, as revealed in their own wills.

Facsimiles are reproduced by permission from the following institutions: The Gerald Coke Handel Collection, The National Archives UK, and The Royal College of Music. I thank the staffs of the institutions concerned for their co-operation in the development of this project, beyond the formal requirement of these permissions. The production of this volume was managed by Katharine Hogg, Librarian of the Gerald Coke Handel Collection; without the support of Hugh Cobbe and the Gerald Coke Handel Foundation this publication would not have been possible. An essential contribution was also made by Terence Best, who provided English translations of French and German texts. Colin Coleman, H. Diack Johnstone and Philip Olleson contributed valuable information that has been incorporated into the essays. To the authors, above all, I extend my thanks for their willing participation, not only in the essays but also in the conversations about the development of this project.

13 The scribe probably began by intending to translate all of the will and codicils into German, but abandoned the task after one page; the third codicil was a curious place to have started, and its significance may have been overrated through the prominence of the name 'Handel' in the first paragraph, if the copyist was specifically looking for references to the German relatives.

Interior view of the Foundling Hospital chapel from the sanctuary. Hand-coloured lithograph by M. & N. Hanhart from the engraving on stone by G.R. Sarjent, [ca.1830]

HANDEL AND HIS WILL

ELLEN T. HARRIS

HANDEL MUST HAVE been pleased at the end of his Lenten oratorio season in 1749. Running from 10 February to 23 March, the season had included the first performances of *Susanna* and *Solomon*, as well as revivals of *Hercules*, *Samson* and *Messiah*, and was one of the strongest programmes that he had ever presented. It was also one of the most lucrative. Between 23 December 1748 and 30 March 1749 he had been able to deposit £2,170 into his cash account at the Bank of England, and the transfer of £2,000 of this to a stock account on 7 April indicates the money was not just revenue, but profit, as Handel at this time purchased stock solely for the purpose of long-term investment. Later in April he added to his public success with the *Music for the Royal Fireworks*. Written to celebrate the Peace of Aix-la-Chapelle ending the War of the Austrian Succession, the *Fireworks Music* was heard first at a rehearsal in Vauxhall Gardens on 21 April before a crowd estimated at about 10,000, and then at Green Park on 25 April.

This relatively new-found professional and financial security – public criticism and financial concerns had troubled him as recently as 1745 – gave Handel the occasion to consider others. On 4 May, less than two weeks after the performance of the *Fireworks music*, he offered a 'Performance of Vocal and Instrumental Music' to the Hospital for the Maintenance and Education of Exposed and Deserted Young Children (the Foundling Hospital), declining an invitation to become a Governor of the Hospital at this time, and choosing rather to 'Serve the Charity with more Pleasure in his Way.'[14] The concert, which took place on 27 May and was attended by the Prince and Princess of Wales, led in the following year to the institution of annual charity performances of *Messiah,* to the great benefit of the Hospital.

These months seem to mark a watershed in Handel's life. At the crest of an extraordinary and long career, having accumulated a substantial personal estate, not to mention a musical legacy that was worth preserving, and with the prospect of his sixty-fifth birthday on 23 February 1750 in view, Handel seems to have begun to think about putting his affairs in order. First, in the month before his birthday, he consolidated his investments, amounting to £7,700, into a single account. Immediately thereafter he must have been immersed in the oratorio season of 1750, which ran from 2 March to 12 April and enabled him, on 19 April, to deposit an additional £1,100 into his stock account. The inaugural charity performance of *Messiah* at the Foundling Hospital followed soon afterwards, on 1 May. Then, on 1 June 1750, Handel wrote his will.

In the eighteenth century wills were often composed only when the testator felt the hand of death upon him, but this seems a far cry from Handel's situation. Although health problems had bothered him in the past, he does not seem to have been dealing with any illness or weakness at the end of the oratorio season in 1750. With the composition of *Theodora* the previous summer he had made a turn from oratorio topics celebrating the political state and national religion (as in *Judas Maccabaeus* and *Solomon*) to personal and reflective subjects focusing on religious freedom and an individual's private relationship with God, a direction that he continued with his next and final oratorio, *Jephtha*, composed in 1751. This introspective turn in Handel's oratorios may, of course, reflect his own preoccupations, but the changed political landscape following the suppression of the Jacobite uprising in 1745 and the Peace of Aix-la-Chapelle in

14 Donald Burrows, *Handel* (Oxford, 1994), p. 299.

1749, two events that imparted a sense of strength and stability to the Hanoverian monarchy, had also reduced the call for works of patriotic fervour.

Seven months after Handel wrote his will, during the composition of *Jephtha*, failing eyesight seriously impeded his work, but there is no previous evidence of this disability. Rather, in February 1750 he had been 'pleasing himself in the purchase of several fine pictures, particularly a large Rembrandt' for his extensive art collection.[15] Further, he made an extended trip to continental Europe in late summer and autumn of 1750, something he might not have undertaken if he had been suffering from serious physical or visual impairments. Perhaps, however, having turned sixty-five and knowing the dangers of long-distance travel, the prospective trip provided an additional impetus to write his will; in the event, he survived a coach accident between The Hague and Haarlem in which he was 'terribly hurt'. Nevertheless, Handel seems to have written his will in 1750 not because his health was endangered, but because he had finally attained the professional security and financial resources to consider doing so, and it is this sense of writing from strength that best characterises the testament.

In his will Handel makes a straightforward declaration in a strong hand. Unlike testators who prepared their wills as death approached, he gives no directions as to his burial, nor, indeed, does he refer to himself at all; his sole purpose is to make bequests to others. Over the next nine years, Handel made four codicils to this will, the first three (on 6 August 1756, 22 March 1757 and 4 August 1757) seemingly prompted by the death of a named legatee. He signed the last codicil (11 April 1759) three days before he died. Only at this final stage did Handel broach the issue of his own burial. Having written a duplicate copy of his will, he must have requested that exact duplicates be made of the codicils as well. In both of the autograph sets the continued erosion of Handel's signature over the five documents gives poignant testimony to his loss of vision.

Although certain conventions were typical of eighteenth-century wills in England, there was no fixed format. They generally began with a religious preamble that included an identification of the testator by parish and county. For example, the will of William Brinck (d. 1771), one of the witnesses who attested to Handel's handwriting during the probate procedure, begins his will:

> In the Name of God Amen I William Brink of Kensington Gore in the Parish of Saint Margaret Westminster in the County of Middlesex Esquire being of Sound Mind and memory Do make this my last Will and Testament in manner following; Viz. First I recommend my Soul into the hands of my Almighty Father who Gave it As to my Body I Desire it may be buryed in a Decent manner but very Private at the Discretion of my Executrix hereinafter named As to the Worldly Estate wherewith it hath pleased God to bless me with I give and Dispose thereof as follows …[16]

In contrast, John Hedges (d. 1737), Treasurer to the Prince of Wales and patron of the painter Joseph Goupy, left a will in rhymed doggerel, without either religious preamble or initial identification of himself. It begins:

> This 5th day of May
> Being Airy and Gay
> To Hipp not enclind
> But of Vigorous mind
> And my Body in Health
> Ile dispose of my Wealth,
> And of all I'm to leave
> On this side of the Grave
> to some one or other –
> I think to my Brother –[17]

Handel's will, in contrast to either of these, steers a middle course that conveys the composer's strong sense of self and also, in some ways, reflects his musical practice: he

Handel House, 1725. Lithograph after a drawing by J.C., ca.1860

15 Donald Burrows and Rosemary Dunhill, *Music and Theatre in Handel's World* (Oxford, 2002), p. 264, letter from the 4th Earl of Shaftesbury to James Harris.
16 The National Archive, PROB 11/971. All subsequent PROB references are from The National Archive.
17 PROB 11/684. On Hedges's patronage of Goupy, see Ellen T. Harris, 'Joseph Goupy and George Frideric Handel: from professional triumphs to personal estrangement', *Huntington Library Quarterly*, 71/3 (2008).

neither snubs convention, nor is he subservient to it. He chooses enough standard wording at the outset to make clear his seriousness of purpose, crafting a concise and authoritative statement of his testamentary wishes that begins 'In the Name of God Amen' and continues that he, 'considering the Uncertainty of human Life[,] doe make this my Will in manner following'. Throughout the will and its four codicils Handel identifies himself by name only ('I George Frideric Handel'), eschewing what would have been the more standard formula: 'I George Frideric Handel of Brook Street in the Parish of St George Hanover Square in the County of Middlesex Esquire'. One senses that he considered his name identification enough, and felt no need to make a declaration of his religious sentiments.

Many testators of this period, in addition to their major legacies, left small bequests for mourning clothes or rings to a wider group of friends and relations. Elizabeth Mayne (d. 1769), one of Handel's own legatees, made a gift of 'a Ring apiece of one Guinea value' to sixteen people, and John Gowland (d. 1776), the apothecary of Bond Street to whom Handel also left a bequest, left 'to each of my Servants that shall be living with me at my decease the Sum of five Pounds for Mourning [clothes]'. Handel makes no such gifts of remembrance, choosing to make only monetary gifts, the smallest of which is £50. This is not to say that Handel was indifferent to how he would be remembered. He provided in his will for the preservation of his musical manuscripts, and in the final codicil he expressed a wish to be buried in Westminster Abbey, leaving £600 for a monument. He seems, however, to have considered personal mourning a matter that could not or should not be dictated from the grave.

The ordering of bequests in the will is also atypical. A married man generally would begin his will with legacies to his wife, moving on to his children, and then to other family and friends, only toward the end of the document making specific cash gifts and presents of clothing to his servants. As Handel never married and his nearest relatives were living in Germany, he appears instead to have organised his list of legatees according to the amount of time that he spent daily with each, moving in order from servants to colleagues, friends, and family.

The first bequest reads: 'I give and bequeath unto my Servant Peter le Blond my Clothes and Linnen, and three hundred Pounds Sterl: and to my other Servants a Year Wages'. LeBlond had probably served as Handel's valet for many years. After his death in 1757 Handel replaced him with his nephew John Duburk, who may have been one of the unnamed servants in this first bequest.[18] As principal servant LeBlond, and later Duburk, would have seen to Handel's personal needs at home and abroad. Duburk, for example, is the highest-paid servant on the personnel list for performances of *Messiah* at the Foundling Hospital in 1758 and 1759.[19] In a similar manner, LeBlond probably attended Handel at performances for many years and may also have travelled with him.

Handel's second bequest gives 'my large Harpsicord, my little House Organ, my Musick Books, and five hundred Pounds Sterl:' to his longstanding professional colleague John Christopher Smith. Born in 1683 as Johann Christoph Schmidt in Kitzingen, Smith met Handel on one of the composer's trips to visit his family in Halle, probably in 1716, and was invited by him to London. He was critically important to Handel, serving as his primary music copyist, and possibly also as orchestral manager and agent for the sale of his works, both in print and in manuscript. No one worked more closely with Handel over a longer period. At times it seems that the two must have sat side by side, Handel passing completed pages to Smith who would transform the composition autograph into a performance copy, a fair-copy 'conducting score' that would be used in the preparation of part-books for the performers and may, indeed, also have been used by Handel in performances as he directed the music from the harpsichord.[20]

Smith's son, also John Christopher Smith, was born in Ansbach in 1712; he and his siblings joined their father in London in 1720. By 1725 Smith junior was studying with Handel and was soon assisting his father. When Handel fell ill in 1737, the younger

18 Little is known of LeBlond, but his name suggests French ancestry, and a Peter LeBlond is listed in the lists of foreign émigrés for 1710: see William Arthur Shaw, *Letters of Denization and Acts of Naturalization for Aliens in England and Ireland, 1603–[1800]*, ii (Huguenot Society of London, xxvii, Manchester, 1923), p. 105. Whether this person was actually Handel's servant cannot be determined, but it does seem likely that LeBlond was a Huguenot (French Protestant), he or his family having fled from French Catholic prosecution. The name Peter LeBlond also appears in the naturalization listing for 9 April 1687, and a Peter LeBlon (*sic*) is listed as the child of Frances and Mary LeBlon on 8 March 1681: see Shaw, *Letters of Denization*, i (Huguenot Society, xviii [London, 1911]), pp. 147, 188.
19 Deutsch, *Handel*, pp. 801, 825.
20 See Hans Dieter Clausen, *Händels Direktionspartituren ('Handexemplare')*, Hamburger Beiträge zur Musikwissenschaft, 7 (Hamburg, 1972), and idem, 'The Hamburg Collection', in Best, *Handel Collections*, pp. 10–28.

Smith substituted for him at the keyboard. While an active composer in his own right, Smith also managed Handel's oratorio performances as the composer's eyesight deteriorated, and had taken over completely by 1754; he continued performing Handel's oratorios in London after the composer's death. It has been thought that Handel vacillated about whether to give his bequest to John Christopher Smith senior or to his son. In the Coke copy of the will the legatee is named as 'Mr. Christopher Smith Senior', but the word 'Senior' is crossed out. Handel made no further clarification, however, and in the probate copy he simply wrote 'Mr. Christopher Smith' as if no additional identification was necessary – which could have been the case if (as seems likely) the senior Smith was known as Christopher and the junior Smith as John (or John Christopher).[21] According to a biography of Smith junior that was published in 1799, Handel quarrelled with Smith senior somewhere around 1755-6 and 'said that he was determined to put his [i.e. Smith junior's] name in place of his father's, in his will',[22] but this cannot explain the amendment made in 1750 and there is no doubt that in 1759 the bequest went to the elder Smith, passing to his son on Smith's death in 1763. Since there appears to be no significant time lapse between the two copies of the will, Handel may simply have eliminated the 'Senior' as redundant and made the correction immediately in the copy, much as would have happened in the copying of his scores.

The next bequest is to James Hunter (b. 1712), named by the eighteenth-century music historian John Hawkins as one of Handel's 'intimate friends'.[23] Hunter descended from two important Huguenot families of merchant traders, the Hunters and the Lannoys, but both his parents died before he turned three years old. The youngest of three orphaned sons, he had no clear promise of support and struck out on his own as a very young man; he married in 1728 at the age of 16 or 17, undoubtedly without the approval of his guardians and extended family. He made his way as a merchant trader for a time, but fell into bankruptcy in 1741. Nevertheless, by 1745 he was able to purchase a dye house in Old Ford, and for the rest of his life profitably sold scarlet-dyed cloth to the East India Company.

Although he earned his living in trade, Hunter's main love seems to have been music. His name appears on subscription lists for Handel's *Alexander's Feast* (1738) and Op. 6 Concerti (1740), and for Boyce's *Solomon* (1743). Hawkins states that 'at great expense [Hunter] had copies made for him of all the music of Handel that he could procure'. This collection can be tentatively associated with the so-called Lennard Collection at the Fitzwilliam Museum. As Donald Burrows has shown, the main body of the collection, begun about 1736, 'was discontinued for some reason in 1741', a date that can now be tied to Hunter's bankruptcy.[24] During his years of financial crisis Hunter himself copied a few of Handel's scores, probably not for the purpose of earning a living but rather to fill the gaps in his own collection for which he could no longer pay, or perhaps to cover the cost of copies that he had already ordered, by work in kind.[25] Hunter's will directed John Walsh, Handel's music publisher, 'to sell ... all the Musick Books', but following his death all of his belongings, including the music books and musical instruments, were auctioned on 30 November 1757 and there is no record of the purchasers.[26]

The most intriguing aspect of the bequest to Hunter in both copies of the will is the obliteration of one phrase that has resisted all efforts to decipher.[27] The ineffectiveness of digital scanning in recovering the deleted text suggests that the cancellation occurred very soon after the wills were written, since there appears to be no distinction between the ink used for the blacking out and the writing underneath. It seems, therefore, not only that both copies of the will were written in close succession, but that Handel's decision to cancel part of the bequest to Hunter occurred quickly thereafter. This much only can be said about the deleted text: as the form of the original bequest would have matched that of the previous two (tangible gifts followed by a monetary gift), the excised portion of Hunter's bequest must have involved one or more objects. Either

---

21 As suggested in Burrows, *Handel*, p. 339 n. 15. Indeed, the elder Smith wrote his will (PROB 11/883) under the name 'Christopher Smith', and his son wrote his (PROB 11/1268) as 'John Christopher Smith'.

22 [William Coxe], *Anecdotes of George Frederick Handel and John Christopher Smith* (London, 1799), p. 48.

23 See Ellen T. Harris, 'James Hunter, Handel's Friend', *Händel-Jahrbuch* 46 (2000), pp. 247-64. The other friend named by Hawkins is Joseph Goupy (see below).

24 Donald Burrows, 'The Barrett Lennard Collection', in Best, *Handel Collections*, pp. 108-37, esp. p. 118.

25 Hunter's hand was for many years identified as that of an anonymous scribe designated 'S7' (see Harris, 'James Hunter', pp. 257-9; also Burrows, '"Something necessary to the connection": Charles Jennens, James Hunter and Handel's *Samson*', *The Handel Institute Newsletter*, 15/1 (2004), pp. 1-3, esp. p. 3 n.9).

26 The auctioneer was Mr Robert Phipps; advertisements for the sale appeared in *The Public Advertiser*, 15 November 1757 and subsequently. The Lennard Collection of manuscript scores of Handel's works can be tentatively associated with John Walsh, the person to whom Hunter bequeathed his collection: see Burrows, 'The Barrett Lennard Collection', pp. 115-17. If indeed Hunter's music books form the basis of this collection, then perhaps Walsh bought them at auction, or if Charles Burney is correct that Walsh purchased a set of manuscript scores of 'almost all the works [Handel] had composed in England' from the composer himself, perhaps Handel or his proxy was the immediate purchaser.

27 The scribe of the 'Register Copy' faithfully reproduced an image of the deleted passage but, as in other such cases, no attempt was made to copy the text which had been crossed out.

Handel had an abrupt change of mind about making the gift at all, or he decided to give the object(s) to Hunter immediately.

The obliteration in the will, and the circumstance that Hunter had predeceased Handel, were both issues that had to be taken up in probate, and both were answered by the servant Duburk. He testified (as found in the affidavit kept with the Probate Copy) that, when the will was located after Handel's death, 'it appeared obliterated in the Bequest therein to Mr James Hunter in the very same Manner and Form as it now appears and the Dep[onen]t further says that he well knew the said James Hunter the Legatee and the said James Hunter died in the Lifetime of the said Mr. Handel the Testator'.

Given this situation, the £500 that Handel had bequeathed to Hunter fell back into the residue of the estate.

Handel concluded the original will with a set of bequests to his family and the appointment of an executor from the family to oversee the distribution of the estate. He gives £100 each to two cousins, Christian Gottlieb Handel and Christian August Rotth, £300 to his cousin Dorothea Elisabeth Taust, a widow, and 'to Her Six Children each two hundred Pounds Sterl[ing]'. Most importantly, he names his niece Johanna Friderica Floercke sole executrix and bequeaths to her the rest and residue (Handel wrote 'next and residue') of his personal estate, specifically mentioning his stock accounts.[28] This bequest contains the only other difference (in addition to the crossed-out 'Senior' in the bequest to John Christopher Smith) between the two autograph copies of the will. In the Coke Copy, Handel first referred to his stock as 'South Sea Annuity's', but crossed this out and wrote instead 'Bank Annuity's 1746. 1 Sub [i.e. first subscription]'. (The text is incomplete on the page in the Coke Collection: the end of the amendment ran over onto the adjoining leaf which has since become separated.) Only the amended version appears in the Probate Copy, again indicating that it was written after the Coke Copy. When writing the Coke Copy, Handel had evidently forgotten that in February 1750 he had consolidated all of his accounts into 4% 1746 Annuities. The mistake is understandable from a number of points of view, but in particular Handel may have thought of his stock accounts as South Sea Annuities in the same way that brand names today are sometimes used as the generic term regardless of manufacturer (as in 'xerox' for 'photocopy'). Handel's first investment after arriving in England had been in South Sea stock, and each time he made new investments he chose South Sea Annuities, only permanently divesting himself of this stock in 1748. At the time of his death, however, the identification of 4% annuities was not accurate either, for on 2 January 1753 he had transferred all of his stock into a 3% consolidated account.

Handel accomplished two important goals in his will. He identified the people for whom he wanted to make provision after his death – his servants, his closest professional colleague, his friend Hunter, and his family – and he established the legal means of enacting his wishes through the creation of the written document and the appointment of an executor. Having achieved these ends in a particularly clear and concise manner, he concluded the will as simply as he had begun: 'In wittness whereof I have hereunto Set my hand this 1 Day of June 1750 ... George Frideric Handel'.

This document stood without alteration for six years. Then in 1756 and 1757 Handel made three separate codicils in quick succession. Although in each case the revision to the will seems to have been prompted by the death of a legatee, he closely follows the order of the original will in making alterations and substitutions, as well as increased bequests. Only thereafter does he take the opportunity to name additional legatees.

He begins the first codicil by increasing Peter LeBlond's bequest from £300 to £500, John Christopher Smith's from £500 to £2,000, and his cousin Christian Gottlieb Handel's from £100 to £300. Although it is impossible to provide a general formula for translating monetary amounts from the eighteenth century into today's currency because the objects in our daily lives have changed so significantly (Handel did not, for example, need to factor in the cost of a car or electricity), one can gain a

John Christopher Smith, by Johann Zoffany (1733-1810)

28 Handel used the feminine form (the addition of the suffix -n or -in) of his niece's surname, writing it as 'Flöerken'; this practice is no longer followed. He did the same thing in dictating the third codicil, by referring to the sister of his cousin as Christiana Susanna Handelin.

general idea if the figures are multiplied by one hundred. In other words, the new bequest to Smith amounted in today's currency to something approximating to £200,000 or $400,000. Handel's generosity was possible because the continued success of his annual oratorio performances from 1750 to 1756 had enabled him almost to double the value of his stock account at the Bank of England from £7,700 in February 1750 to £15,000 (or about £1,500,000 today) in June 1756. Even these figures probably underestimate the modern equivalent values.

His cousin Christian August Rotth having died, in this first codicil Handel transferred the legacy to his widow, and doubled it from £100 to £200. He also planned for the contingency of her death, stating that 'if she shall die before me, I give the said Two Hundred Pounds to her Children'. As his cousin Dorothea Elisabeth Taust and one of her children had also died in the meantime, he redistributed their legacies, increasing his bequests to the five surviving children from £200 to 'Three Hundred Pounds apiece'. Handel also added two new bequests, recognising the contributions of two of his oratorio librettists. Thomas Morell, a doctor of divinity who held various posts during his lifetime and 'supplemented his income with a variety of publications', had been Handel's librettist for *Judas Maccabaeus* (first performed in 1747), *Alexander Balus* (1748), *Theodora* (1750) and *Jephtha* (1752);[29] Handel left him £200. Newburgh Hamilton, who received £100, served as steward to the Earl of Strafford and had prepared for Handel important adaptations of texts by John Dryden and John Milton: *Alexander's Feast* (1736), *Samson* (1743) and the *Occasional Oratorio* (1746).[30]

Handel's failing eyesight made it impossible for him to undertake the task of preparing this codicil on his own. For assistance in this matter it seems most likely that he appealed to his friend Thomas Harris, who had been called to the Bar at Lincoln's Inn and was a Master in Chancery, and it was probably Harris who engaged John Hetherington, a lawyer of Middle Temple and clerk in the First-Fruits Office (which oversaw the taxation of income to clergy), as scribe. Hetherington not only had the correct professional qualifications, but Handel knew him, which would have been a comfort. Only a few months before, on 29 May 1756, Hetherington and Harris had been at the London house of Charles Jennens, a patron of the arts and another of Handel's librettists (see below), when the composer had recounted events from early in his life and, although blind, played on Jennens's forte-piano.[31] In preparing the codicil, a process that may have taken a number of days, Handel must have laid out his intentions, after which Hetherington would have used his own notes to draw up the document. On 6 August 1756 this was 'read over to the said George Frideric Handel and was by him Sign'd and Publish'd in our Presence', as stated in the declaration appended to the codicil, which was then countersigned by Harris and Hetherington, presumably on the same occasion.

One of the most important revisions in this codicil was the addition of 'George Amyand Esquire of Lawrence Pountney Hill[,] London[,] Merchant[,] Co-executor with my Niece mention'd in my Will'. This change may have been recommended by Harris, as it would have been difficult, perhaps impossible, for Johanna Floercke to oversee the execution of the will from Halle. Amyand, of Huguenot descent, was an eminent banker and merchant trader. A Member of Parliament for Barnstaple from 1754, he was created baronet in 1764.[32] Harris and Amyand may have been personally acquainted. In 1765 'Mr Emyand' (probably George Amyand's brother) is listed among the guests at the London home of Thomas Harris's older brother James, and in 1777 Amyand's youngest daughter married Thomas Harris's nephew James Harris (that is, the son of his brother James), later first Earl of Malmesbury.[33] In addition to making Amyand a co-executor, Handel gave him 'Two Hundred Pounds which I desire him to Accept for the Care and Trouble he shall take in my affairs'.

Handel had a single purpose in preparing the second codicil (22 March 1757): to take account of the death of 'my Old Servant Peter LeBlond'. He put LeBlond's

---

29 Ruth Smith, 'Morell, Thomas (1703-1784)', in *The Oxford Dictionary of National Biography* (Oxford 2004 and subsequent online eds, hereafter *ODNB*).

30 Winton Dean and Ruth Smith, 'Hamilton, Newburgh', in *The New Grove Dictionary of Music and Musicians*, 2nd ed. (London, 2001) and subsequent online eds as *Grove Music Online*.

31 See Burrows and Dunhill, *Music and Theatre*, p. 314, for the diary entry of George Harris, younger brother of Thomas, concerning the party at Jennens's house; pp. 1102-6, for short biographies of Thomas Harris, Hetherington and Jennens, and *passim* for Harris's interactions with Handel. See also Donald Burrows, 'Handel and the Pianoforte', in Hans Joachim Marx (ed.), *Göttinger Händel-Beiträge*, ix (2002), pp. 123-42.

32 Amyand's familial and mercantile connections in Hamburg probably played a role in his choice as executor. See Sir Lewis Namier and John Brooke, *The House of Commons 1754-1790*, (3 vols, London, 1964), ii, pp. 20-21, and George E. Cokayne, *Complete Baronetage*, (6 vols, Exeter, 1900-1909), v, p. 130. It has sometimes been suggested that Amyand's ancestry was Jewish, but this seems to be an error. Concerning Amyand's older brother Claudius Amyand, see Romney Sedgwick, *The House of Commons 1715-1754* (2 vols, London, 1970), i, p. 414.

33 For 'Emyand', see Burrows and Dunhill, *Music and Theatre*, p. 439. Although James Harris senior (1709-1780) is not among the legatees in Handel's will, he was an important patron of the composer, the author of the first draft of the libretto for Handel based on Milton's poems *L'Allegro* and *Il Penseroso*, which Jennens completed, and the owner of the manuscript scores of Handel's music, now known as the Malmesbury Collection, which had originally been copied for Elizabeth Legh between 1715 and 1734: for all of these topics, and further details of the Harris family, see *Music and Theatre*.

nephew John Duburk in his place as the recipient of a £500 legacy, and raised the next underservant, Thomas Bramwell, to a named position in the will with a bequest of 'Thirty Pounds in Case He shall be living with me at the time of my death and not otherways'. Beginning with the first bequest of his original will, Handel had recognised and rewarded the assistance of his servants. Now that his blindness made their continual help essential, he apparently updated his will on their account alone. Once again Hetherington wrote out the document, and he and Thomas Harris witnessed it.

For the third codicil (4 August 1757) Hetherington appears not to have been available, so a John Maxwell (who cannot be positively identified) joined Harris as a witness and substituted for Hetherington as scribe (would that his hand was as clear). Christian Gottlieb Handel, to whom Handel had left £300, had died, so the composer now bequeathed £300 apiece to Christian Gottlieb's sisters (Christiana Susanna and Rahel Sophia). He also made some tangible gifts, clarifying the ownership of things currently in his possession or purchased by himself. To John Rich, the manager of the theatres at Lincoln's Inn Fields and Covent Garden, he left 'my Great Organ that stands at the Theatre Royal in Covent Garden'. This was presumably the organ that Handel had purchased in 1745 for the King's Theatre, which had probably been adapted for Covent Garden in the following year.34 To Charles Jennens, who had provided Handel with the librettos for *Saul* (first performed in 1739), *L'Allegro, il Penseroso ed il Moderato* (1740), *Messiah* (1742), *Belshazzar* (1745) and, probably, *Israel in Egypt* (1739), he gave 'two pictures, the Old Man's head and the Old Woman's head done by Denner'. And to his friend Bernard Granville, he left 'the Landskip [landscape], a view of the Rhine, done by Rembrand, & another Landskip said to be done by the same hand which he made me a Present of some time ago'. A distinctive aspect of this codicil is its indication that Handel was having some difficulty remembering names, or in communicating them to an amanuensis. The Earl of Shaftesbury had written to James Harris in a letter of February 1757 that 'Handel's memory is strengthened of late to an astonishing degree', but in this document the composer identifies only one of his female cousins, Christiana Susanna, by name, referring to the other as the 'Sister living at Pless near Teschen in Silesia'.35 The codicil also leaves a blank space for Bernard Granville's first name.

The tangible gifts give further evidence of an attribute of Handel's will that seems congruent with the priority that he gives his servants. By and large, those who have ample means of their own do not receive monetary gifts, which would explain why Handel left cash bequests to his oratorio librettists Morell and Hamilton, but not to Jennens and some others. Rich's profits from Covent Garden were considerable, while Granville and Jennens, both avid collectors of Handel's music as well as of art, were independently wealthy.36 The composer also enjoyed collecting art: the inventory of his collection auctioned after his death (which did not, of course, contain the two portraits by Balthasar Denner or the two landscapes said to be by Rembrandt that he had bequeathed by will) contains 80 paintings.37

The final bequest in this third codicil is the gift of 'a fair copy of the Score and all the parts of my Oratorio called *The Messiah* to the Foundling Hospital'. Handel had by then been presenting annual charity performances of *Messiah* at the Foundling Hospital for eight years, and in 1754 the Hospital had sought to preserve the 'great Benefit' they had received from these performances by asking the composer to initiate an Act of Parliament that would grant them proprietary rights to *Messiah*.38 Handel refused, but his bequest of a score and 'all the parts' gave the Hospital the performing material that would be needed to continue the concerts after his death. In the event this material, specially copied for the Hospital, was not used, because the performers continued to use their old music copies.

The last codicil (11 April 1759) differs from the preceding ones in not having been necessitated by the deaths of named legatees, but rather by Handel's own failing health.

Thomas Morell, artist unknown, after a print by James Basire (1762) after a drawing by Hogarth

34 Burrows, *Handel*, pp. 282-4.
35 For Shaftesbury's letter, see Burrows and Dunhill, *Music and Theatre*, p. 321.
36 See Ruth Smith, 'Jennens, Charles (1700/01-1773)' in *ODNB*; John Roberts, 'The Aylesford Collection', in Best, *Handel Collections*, pp. 39-86 [on Jennens's collection]; and Burrows, 'The "Granville" and "Smith" Collections of Handel's Manuscripts', in Chris Banks, Arthur Searle and Malcolm Turner (eds), *Sundry Sorts of Music Books: Essays on the British Library Collections, presented to O. W. Neighbour on his 70th Birthday* (London, 1993), pp. 231-47.
37 Jacob Simon, 'Handel's Collection of Paintings', in Jacob Simon (ed.), *Handel: A Celebration of his Life and Times, 1685-1759* (London, 1985), pp. 289-90; Alison Meyric Hughes and Martin Royalton-Kisch, 'Handel's Art Collection', *Apollo*, 146 (1997), pp. 17-23.
38 See Donald Burrows, 'Handel and the Foundling Hospital', *Music & Letters*, 58/3 (July 1977), pp. 278-9.

From harmony, from heavenly harmony. Engraving by Francesco Bartolozzi after the drawing by Giovanni Battista Cipriani, 1784

Signed three days before he died, it is his death-bed testament. Consistent with the will and prior codicils, he again remembered those who had done him service. He adjusted the gifts to his servants, leaving all of his wearing apparel to Duburk (written here as Le Bourk), a provision that he had previously made for his late servant LeBlond; increasing the bequest to Thomas Bramwell (who apparently had continued to live with Handel – see the third codicil) by £70 to a total of £100; and giving to his 'two Maid Servants each one years Wages over and above what shall be due to them at the time of my death'. He doubled the bequest to Amyand to £400 and added gifts for Hetherington (£100) and Thomas Harris (£300). For the first time he gave general consideration to his musical colleagues. He made a munificent gift of £1000 to the Fund for Decayed Musicians, to support musicians and their families in need, which was administered by the Society of Musicians.[39] In 1738 Handel had been one of the founders of this Society (which continues today as The Royal Society of Musicians of Great Britain), and from its inception he had taken part in annual concerts for the benefit of the Fund. He also made a separate bequest to the violinist Matthew Dubourg, who had led the orchestra during the Dublin season of 1741–42 which included the first performances of *Messiah*, and had arranged performances of Handel's music in Dublin after that time; he had also led the orchestra for Handel's London oratorio season in 1743.

Next, he focused on former and current neighbours. These bequests open what has otherwise been a closed door, making it possible to trace a number of Handel's social connections in London and revealing a network of interrelationships between his friends and associates. The largest gift (£500) among this group of beneficiaries went to James Smyth, the owner of a perfumery on New Bond Street. That he was a friend can be assumed, but Handel may also have used his professional services, for perfumers were at this time closely aligned with both personal grooming and pharmaceuticals. Smyth was one of the last people from outside the composer's household to see him before his death on 14 April. In a letter to Bernard Granville informing him that 'on Saturday last died the great and good Mr. Handel', he described the composer's last days:

> He took leave of all his friends on Friday morning, and desired to see nobody but the Doctor and Apothecary and myself. At 7 o'clock in the evening he took leave of me and told me we 'would meet again'; as for that he had *now done with the world*.[40]

The apothecary referred to was probably John Gowland, also of New Bond Street, who had been apothecary to the Prince of Wales from about 1741 to the time of his death in 1751. Handel acknowledged him with a gift of £50. Another legatee, John Belchier of Sun Court, Threadneedle Street, an eminent surgeon at Guy's Hospital, may have been the doctor; however, as he was also a friend, Handel's bequest of 'Fifty Guineas' could have been an acknowledgment of this friendship.[41] Twenty-five years later, Charles Burney asserted that Richard Warren, a distinguished physician who had worked at Middlesex Hospital, had attended the composer in his final illness.[42] Dr Warren does not appear in Handel's will, but he lived nearby; as he was appointed physician to George III in 1762, he may also have had a professional association with Gowland, who was made apothecary to George III in the same year. Handel also made a gift of 50 guineas to Benjamin Martyn who, like Smyth and Gowland, lived in New Bond Street. Martyn was a writer who served as secretary to the Board of Trustees for establishing the colony of Georgia and was employed by the fourth Earl of Shaftesbury to write a biography of the first Earl. As a friend of Handel's, he was a useful source of advance information about the oratorio seasons: in 1757 Thomas Harris needed to 'send to Mr. Martyn to know Handel's scheme of performances'.[43]

This codicil seems to flow largely as stream-of-consciousness, with additions as Handel remembered them. Following the gifts to musicians, his male servants, and friends (not separately categorised as before, but intermixed), and with a sense of conclusion, he turns to his own burial. Then, rather abruptly, he appears to remember the

---

39 The full title was 'The Fund for the Support of Decayed Musicians and their Families'.
40 Deutsch, *Handel*, pp. 818–19.
41 A guinea was worth 21 shillings, and was thus more valuable than a pound (20 shillings). Belchier, a mutual friend of Handel and the poet Alexander Pope, had tried unsuccessfully to persuade the composer to set Pope's *Ode for Music*: see Charles Burney, *An Account of the Musical Performances ... in Commemoration of Handel* (London, 1785), 'Sketch of the Life of Handel' p. 33.
42 Burney, *An Account*, 'Sketch' p. 31.
43 Burrows and Dunhill, *Music and Theatre*, p. 321.

women in his life, grouping his maid servants together with women of greater social standing, as he had done with the comparable male legatees earlier in the codicil. Finally, his gift of £200 to Mr Reiche, 'Secretary for the affairs of Hanover', was probably made, as with so many of the bequests, in gratitude for both friendship and professional assistance. It recalls Handel's connection with the House of Hanover that was almost of fifty years' standing, through Kings George I and George II in London, and back to his appointment to the Electoral Court at Hanover itself in 1710.

Among Handel's female legatees, the first bequest is to 'Mrs. Palmer of Chelsea, Widow of Mr. Palmer, formerly of Chappel Street, One Hundred Pounds'. Elizabeth Palmer (née Peacock, b. 1722-d. after 1764) was the widow of Ralph [Raphe] Palmer, the third-generation person to carry this name. Her parents had been servants, and the Palmers legally separated her from the family inheritance so that her husband could only leave her a life interest (but with permission to sell any of his estate) on his death in 1755.[44] From the time of their marriage in 1747 they lived in a large house in Curzon Street, within Handel's parish of St George, Hanover Square. Palmer was an avid collector of art and books, but much of the collection, like the house itself, was sold by Elizabeth after his death, presumably in order to raise sufficient money to secure a stable income. Significant items from Palmer's collection can still be traced.[45] After her husband died Elizabeth moved to the corner of Park Street and Chappel Street (now Alford Street), and then to Chelsea.[46] The nature of Handel's specific association with the Palmers is unknown.

After leaving an additional bequest to his two (unnamed) maids, Handel adds two further bequests to women: 50 Guineas each to 'Mrs. Mayne of Kensington Widow Sister of the late Mr. Batt' and 'Mrs. Donnalan of Charles Street Berkley Square'. Elizabeth Mayne (née Batt, 1695-1768) married John Mayne, Lord of the Manor of Teffont Evias, Wiltshire, in 1722. As the Batt family was part of the social circle of the Harrises in Salisbury, she might have met her husband in those environs. After he died in 1726, leaving her with two young children, she divided her time between Wiltshire and the Batt family residence in Kensington. Handel had probably met Mrs Mayne through her brother, Christopher Batt, who died in 1756. According to family tradition, Mayne befriended Handel 'at the time of his persecution', probably in the early 1740s when he faced significant public opposition.[47] She was a skilled harpsichordist; her childhood music book survives in the British Library, meticulously labeled 'Elizabeth Batt 1704' in Gothic script.[48]

Anne Donnellan (?1700-1762) was a close friend of Mary Delany (née Granville, later Pendarves, 1700-1788), the sister of Bernard Granville, through whom she undoubtedly met the composer.[49] After the death of her father Nehemiah Donnellan, Lord Chief Baron of the Exchequer of Ireland (d. 1705), her mother had married Philip Perceval (brother to John, later first Earl of Egmont), and it was he who brought the family to London in the late 1720s. Mrs Delany's later correspondence records a number of social events (at all of their houses) at which she, Donnellan and Handel were present.[50] Anne Donnellan had a fine reputation as an amateur singer: Lord Orrery warned the Bishop of Cork in 1736 not to be surprised if Lord Burlington 'quits his Nitch' and 'flings himself at Miss Donallan's Feet as soon as ever "Verdi prati" [from Handel's *Alcina*] reach his ears'.[51] Donnellan never married (the title of Mrs was used for women above a certain age, like 'Madame' in French); at her death she left to the British Museum a miniature portrait of Handel by Rupert Barber.[52]

Like the first and second codicils, this last codicil appears to have been written out by John Hetherington, but neither he nor Thomas Harris served as witnesses. The likely reason for their abstention is that they were both named for bequests in the codicil, although the use of legatees as witnesses was not at all uncommon. John Christopher Smith the younger signed as one witness; the other is an unidentified person named Rudd.[53]

[44] The information on the Peacock family comes from a note dated 11 February 1747 written by Ralph Verney, first Earl Verney and first cousin to Ralph Palmer, on the back of a letter to him (British Library microfilm of letters of the Verney family, Claydon House). The legal documents concerning the disposition of the Palmer real estate are in East Sussex Record Office, FRE 8353-8364, and the Chancery copy of Ralph Palmer's will survives at PROB 11/814.

[45] Examples include Rembrandt's *Man in Oriental Costume* (Metropolitan Museum of Art, New York) and an illuminated Bible from the second half of the thirteenth century (British Library: Burney 2).

[46] The rate-books from St George, Hanover Square, now at the City of Westminster Archives Centre, identify the Palmer residences in the parish.

[47] Sir Richard Colt Hoare, *The History of Modern Wiltshire* (6 vols, London, 1822-1844), iv, p. 112.

[48] British Library, Add. MS. 52363.

[49] On Donnellan, see Patrick Kelly, 'Anne Donnellan: Irish proto-Bluestocking', in *Hermathena: A Trinity College Dublin Review*, 154 (1993), pp. 39-68.

[50] *The Autobiography and Correspondence of Mary Granville, Mrs. Delany*, ed. Augusta Waddington Hall, Lady Llanover (6 vols, London, 1861-2).

[51] *The Orrery Papers*, ed. Countess of Cork and Orrery (2 vols, London, 1903), i, p. 177.

[52] A record of the gift dated 11 June 1762 is found in the 'Department of Antiquities and Coins. Donations 1756-1836' at the British Museum, Medieval and Later Antiquities Department; the portrait itself is now lost. The Chancery copy of Donnellan's will survives (PROB 11/875).

[53] In modern transcriptions of the will Rudd's initials are usually given as A. J., but the Chancery scribe in 1759 wrote A. S. If the contemporary scribe was correct, as seems likely, this witness might possibly be the Samuel Rudd who appears in 1755 as a recorder in short-hand at the Old Bailey court (*The Public Advertiser*, 27 January 1755).

With death in view, Handel asked 'permission of the Dean and Chapter of Westminster to be buried in Westminster Abbey' and requested that 'his Executor may have leave to erect a Monument for me there', making provision for a sum of up to £600 to cover its cost. He further requested that his burial should take place 'in a private manner'. On the day Handel died Amyand paid £45 5s. 6d. towards the 'Fees for the Funeral of George Frederick Handel Esq:ʳ in the South Cross of Westminster Abby'; charges that were paid later include 6 guineas for a gravestone and further payments of £17 17s. 2d. and £3 in fees to the clergy.[54] The funeral took place on 20 April, and 'though he had mentioned being privately interred, yet, from the respect due to so celebrated a man, the Bishops, Prebends and the whole Choir attended'.[55] It was estimated that 'there were not fewer than 3000 Persons present on this Occasion'.[56] The French émigré sculptor Louis François Roubiliac, whose statue of Handel erected at Vauxhall Gardens in 1737 was among his first works for London, was commissioned to create the monument; it turned out to be his last work. Roubiliac is said to have taken a death mask of Handel to serve as his model for the sculpture, which Hawkins described as 'the most perfect resemblance [in which] the true lineaments of his face are apparent'.[57] The Dean and Chapter of Westminster were paid an additional fee of £25 for a site for the monument, but no record survives of payment to Roubiliac, who died on 11 January 1762.[58] The monument was dedicated on 15 July 1762.

On the day of Handel's death, which was Holy Saturday (the day before Easter Sunday), Amyand not only took care of arranging Handel's funeral but also appeared before the Prerogative Court at Doctors' Commons to swear to the 'Truth of this Will and to the several Codicils hereunto annext'. On 22 April two more witnesses appeared personally to testify that 'they very well knew George Frideric Handell … and are well acquainted w[i]th his Manner and Character of handwriting having often seen him write … [and] that they do verily beleive the whole Body and Contents of the said Will and the s[ai]d Name George Frideric Handel thereto subscribed to be all of the proper handwriting of the said George Frideric Handel Esq.ʳ deceased'.

Both men, William Brinck Esquire of the Parish of St James Westminster, and Edward Cavendish, Gentleman of the Parish of Paddington, must have had regular dealings with Handel, probably in a professional or mercantile capacity, but whatever these might have been is unknown today.[59] Finally, on 24 April Duburk testified to the discovery of the will and its codicils 'locked and sealed up together' in Handel's bureau, to the obliteration found at that time in the bequest to James Hunter, and to the death of Hunter before Handel. On 26 April probate was granted to Amyand with the 'power reserved to make the like grant to Johanna Friderica Floercken … when she shall apply for the same'. The official registration of Probate at the Bank of England on 30 April then cleared the way for Amyand to begin paying out the bequests from Handel's account. The first, on 2 May, was to [John] Christopher Smith for £2,470.

Stock accounts at the Bank of England were not recorded in cash value but rather at a fixed (par) value of £100. The actual value fluctuated with the market, so it is necessary to find the trading price on any specific day to know the cash value of an account. During the period that Amyand made payments from this account, from 2 May to 31 October 1759, consolidated 3% annuities were selling under par at about £80, and thus the cash value of the £17,500 of stock in Handel's account was about £14,000.[60] Trading value for the annuity closed at 80¾ on 2 May, and at this price the £2,470 in annuities transferred to Smith would have approximated (at £1994 10s.) to the bequest of £2,000, but if Amyand actually sold the stock at a value of 81, which could easily have happened over the course of the day, it would have equalled £2,000. Similar accounting needs to be done for payouts to other named legatees, such as Duburk and James Smyth.

Many of the recipients of stock, however, are not named legatees. The payout to 'Peter Gillier Senior & Co.' refers not to a personal legacy, but to authorised agents for the Society of Musicians, whose minutes record that the £1,254 'of the reduced Bank

---

54 The Dean and Chapter of Westminster, Fee Book, p. 125v; Simon, *Handel*, p. 233.
55 *The Universal Chronicle*, 28 April 1759; Deutsch, *Handel*, p. 821.
56 *The London Evening-Post*, 24 April 1759; Deutsch, *Handel* p. 821.
57 Simon, *Handel*, p. 47.
58 Simon, *Handel*, p. 47; Malcolm Baker, 'Roubiliac, Louis François (1702–1762)', *ODNB*.
59 Brinck's will, proved on 2 October 1771 and cited above, indicates a man of some wealth. He left £1,000 apiece to a sister-in-law and her daughter, and the residue of his estate to his sister.
60 See Harris, 'Handel the Investor', for a full description of these accounts and the trading prices on specific days.

Annuities, now standing in the names of Mr. Thomas Wood, Mr. Peter Gillier, and Mr. Christian Reich, in the books of the company of the Bank of England', were transferred to them by Amyand 'in full satisfaction and discharge of the Legacy of One Thousand Pounds, given and bequeathed by the said George Frederic Handel': that is, £1,254 of 3% annuities sold at 79¾ equalled £1,000.[61] Some of the other recipients may also have been proxies. As is the case with Handel's stock accounts during his life, most of the names can be identified as brokers to whom Amyand probably sold the stock for cash. Since some of the people named in Handel's will did not hold stock accounts at the Bank of England, which would have been necessary for a stock transfer, they must have been paid in currency.

On 19 September 1759 the Taust family in Halle sent a bill of exchange to Amyand for the payment of the bequest that Handel had left them. Amyand refused payment, however, since it was drawn for £1,500 rather than £1,200 (10 October 1759). The issue seems to have been that the Tausts read Handel's bequest of £300 to each of the five living children at the time of the first codicil in 1756 as a gift *per stirpes* (that is, as a total gift of £1,500 to be divided among any living children of his cousin Dorothea Elisabeth Taust), whereas Amyand read it as a gift *per capita*, or £300 to each living child, of which there were four at the time of Handel's death, with the amount bequeathed to any child who predeceased Handel falling into the residue bequeathed to Handel's niece (as was also the case with the lapsed bequest to Hunter).

The resolution of the disagreement with the Taust family is not entirely clear, but Amyand appears not to have countenanced any further discussion. On 11 October he transferred £9,000 into an account for Johanna Friderica Floercke. This amount probably represents all of the money sent to Germany, with Floercke in her designated, if not sworn, role of executrix acting as proxy for Handel's family. At a trading value of £82 (on 12 October the annuity was selling at 82¼), this amount of stock would have been worth £7,380. If the bequests of £200 to the Rotth family, £600 to the sisters of Christian Gottlieb Handel, and £1,200 to the Taust family are subtracted from the cash value of the stock transfer, £5,380 is left as a cash bequest to Handel's niece.

The cash bequests from Handel's will, not including the 'residue' to Floercke or the gift to Hunter, total £8,450, or about £10,562 of stock at a selling price of £80. Adding this to the £9,000 of stock transferred to Floercke would require £19,562 of stock. But if the £2,000 in bequests to family is subsumed in this payment, then the remaining cash bequests total only £6,450, or about £8,062 of stock. If this is added to Floercke's £9,000 the total sum becomes £17,062 and that amount, given the fluctuations in price, closely matches the £17,500 of stock in Handel's account at the time of his death. Once the cash bequests were disbursed, additional currency would have been needed for payment of the servants' wages, as Handel willed, as well as any outstanding debts and funeral costs. These expenses could have been met in part from the sale of stock, and from the sale of Handel's household goods and art collection, but there was probably also some additional money that had been kept in the house or in a cash account with a neighbouring merchant.[62] On Wednesday 31 October Amyand closed the account at the Bank of England with transfers to three non-legatees, two of whom can positively be identified as brokers; probably all three transfers resulted in cash that was used to complete the execution of Handel's will.

Handel's will provides us with insights into Handel the man. Its direct and concise wording reflects his straightforward, and sometimes blunt, manner. He was not a man for superficial niceties: as so often in his music, he cuts directly to the heart of the matter. What is not included is also important. For example, Handel is said to have altered his intention to leave a bequest to Joseph Goupy, formerly a close friend, after the artist drew and published a vicious caricature of the composer. An anecdote printed in 1776 about this incident claims that Handel would not forgive Goupy because he had 'abused his Friendship' and endeavored to give his patrons 'an ill Impression of him'.[63]

Handel, attributed to the school of Thomas Hudson

61 Deutsch, *Handel*, pp. 827-8.
62 Handel's remaining household goods (see note 5, above) were bought by Duburk for £48 on 7 August 1759, and his art collection was auctioned by Mr Langford on 28 February 1760. A copy of the sale catalogue of the art collection is in the Frick Art Library, New York: see Simon, *Handel*, pp. 289-90, also Hugh McLean, 'Bernard Granville, Handel and the Rembrandts', *The Musical Times*, 126/10 (October 1985), pp. 593-601..
63 *The St. James's Chronicle; Or, British Evening-Post*, 20-22 August 1776, 'Anecdote of Handel', p. 1.

View of Handel Monument in Westminster Abbey. Engraving by Jean-Marie Delattre after a drawing by E.F. Burney

Whether or not these statements actually represent Handel's words, they certainly reflect the priorities of his will: to honour his family and friends, to acknowledge those who had assisted him in various ways, to maintain the stability of those charities he had been engaged with during his life, and to assure his musical legacy.

The will also illustrates Handel's general adherence to the custom of having capital and responsibility pass down chronologically and from male to female. John Duburk receives a bequest following the death of his uncle, but is not named previously when his uncle, especially if they were working together, was his senior. Similarly, Handel's legacy to the Rotth family passes first from the father to the mother and then to the children. His gift to John Christopher Smith, understood in this context, seems even more clearly to point to Smith senior, something that Handel first makes explicit and then takes as understood. It may also be that this practice lies behind his gifts to Mrs Mayne and Mrs Palmer, both of whom are identified by the male relative who would traditionally have taken fiscal responsibility for them. Mayne's husband had died in 1726 and, given his residence in Teffont Evias, it is unlikely Handel knew him, but it is probable that he knew her brother Christopher Batt as well as Palmer's husband Ralph. His gifts to these women may, therefore, be understood in some sense as transferred bequests from their late male protectors. The exclusion from the will of Mary Delany, a known friend and supporter of Handel, may speak to the same issue. Not only was she living in Ireland at the time of Handel's death, and therefore out of Handel's immediate neighbourhood, but she was also a married woman and Handel had made her brother Bernard Granville, equally a close friend, a legatee.

These cultural norms did not, however, dominate Handel's will, as they did those of so many others. Rather, they exist in parallel to, and sometimes in competition with, his own extraordinary sense of responsibility and charity. Factors governing Handel's choice of legatees included type of income (he favoured those who earned their living, however wealthy) and geographical proximity to him during his last years. For example, he did not leave a gift of any type for James Harris, who lived in Salisbury and had inherited wealth, but he did mark his gratitude to Harris's younger brother Thomas (a prosperous London lawyer) who had assisted him with his will. He acknowledges the contributions of three of his oratorio librettists by making monetary or tangible bequests based on the stability of their income and their proximity to him at the time of his death. That he left nothing to Thomas Broughton, who compiled the text of *Hercules*, may have been primarily because he no longer lived in London; in addition, he held a good position within the church. It is interesting to note that although Handel supports the Fund for Decayed Musicians and leaves a monetary bequest to the violinist Dubourg, he leaves nothing to any of his singers. Some of these, for example Susanna Cibber and John Beard, had more than adequate means of support, but Handel may also have felt that, unlike his librettists or orchestral musicians, his solo singers had received due acknowledgment from the public.

Handel's request to be buried in Westminster Abbey and to have a significant monument erected in his memory certainly speaks to his sense of self, which although strong was not misplaced. More important than the burial or monument, however, was the bequest of his 'Musick Books' to John Christopher Smith, making it possible, at least in the short term, to perpetuate performances of his music after his death. His autograph manuscripts then passed from father to son, undoubtedly in a way that Handel would have anticipated, and their subsequent gift from the younger Smith to George III preserved them for posterity. Although Handel's important charitable legacies continue today in the work of the Royal Society of Musicians and in frequent benefit performances of *Messiah* worldwide, his greatest bequest to future generations was surely the preservation of his music. In our receipt of this gift, we have all become legatees of the 'great and good Mr. Handel'.

HANDEL'S GERMAN RELATIVES

KLAUS-PETER KOCH

In order to understand Handel's relationship to the various family members named in his will, we have to begin with his father. Georg Händel (baptised in Halle on 24 September 1622, died there 14 February 1697) was a professional gentleman, usually described as a surgeon and barber. The German terms Bader, Barbier (= barber), Wundarzt and Chirurg (= surgeon) go back to differentiations that began within the medical profession during the Middle Ages. The Bader runs a 'Badestube', but also deals with illnesses, including the care of teeth and eyes, and surgery: he can draw teeth, administer enemas, and perform procedures involving 'bleeding' and the drawing of blood with leeches.[64] The Barbier (sometimes an assistant to a Bader, but otherwise an independent practitioner, as was the case with Georg Händel) is likewise based in the Badestube: he is not only a hairdresser and beard-trimmer, but also a medical doctor with similar professional competence to the Bader in dentistry, ophthalmology and surgery. The Wundarzt is an early equivalent of the modern surgeon: as town doctors they were called Stadtphysikus, and in military service Feldscher. Handel's father held appointments as 'Geheimer Cammerdiener und Leib-chirurgo' and 'Cammerdiener und Chirurgus von Haus aus' to the Saxon and Brandenburg courts that successively administered Halle. ('Cammerdiener' was his status within the court hierarchy, and 'Chirurgus' his professional role.) He also had a similar post at Weissenfels, to which the Saxon court had moved when Halle was handed over to Brandenburg in 1680.

On 20 February 1643 Georg Händel married the widow Anna Oettinger: she had been born about 1610-11 and died in 1682, a victim of the virulent plague in Halle at that time. Now a widower, Händel re-married, on 23 April 1683. His second wife, Dorothea Elisabeth Taust, had been born in Dieskau (a place to the south-east of Halle) in 1651 and died in Halle on 27 December 1730. She was the daughter of the parish priest of the nearby village of Giebichenstein, where Georg Händel had been the local doctor (Amtchirurg) since 1645.[65] From the first marriage there were three sons and three daughters; from the second, two sons (including Georg Friedrich) and two daughters.[66] By the time Handel's mother died in 1730, all of his siblings and half-siblings were already dead. To identify the members of his family to whom he made bequests, we have therefore to look to the next generations, and to more distant relationships of descendants from these brothers and sisters. The 'cousin Christian Gottlieb Handel' named as the first family legatee in Handel's will (and in the first codicil) was a grandson of Carl Handel, a half-brother from his father's first marriage – the only one, in fact, to be still alive when Handel was born. Carl was born in 1649, so he was more than 35 years older than George Frideric, but nevertheless they may have had quite a cordial relationship.[67] He had followed his father's profession and was 'Kammerdiener und Leib-Barbier' to Duke Johann Adolf I of Sachsen-Weissenfels, the Saxon court that had formerly been in Halle. According to anecdotes in Mainwaring's biography, Handel's father was persuaded (with considerable reluctance) to allow his young son to join him on a visit to Weissenfels, specifically so that he could meet this half-brother, and it was Carl who revealed to the Duke the identity of the young organist who was heard playing in the court chapel, thus prompting the beginning of

---

64 The literal translation of 'Badestube' is 'Bath-house': there were facilities for body cleaning and cosmetics, but for the administration of personal care the Badestube also functioned as a medical surgery.

65 At the time Giebichenstein was an independent place, about a mile from the northern boundary of Halle; it was incorporated into the city in 1900.

66 For details of those relatives who were not relevant to Handel's bequests, see Klaus-Peter Koch, 'Handel's Family', *The Handel Institute Newsletter*, 19/2 (Autumn 2008); for diagrams of the 'family tree' see Burrows, *Handel*, pp. 4–5.

67 Carl was baptised on 30 September 1649 in Neumarkt, a suburb just to the north of Halle, outside the city walls and administratively separate. All of the children from Georg Händel's first marriage were baptised there.

Handel with a score of Messiah. English school after a portrait by Francis Kyte

Handel's musical training.[68] Carl died at Weissenfels and was buried there on 5 April 1713.

In 1672 Carl Handel had married Justina Margaretha Franckenberger at Langensalza, a town in Thuringia north-west of Erfurt, where her father was Rätskammerer (treasurer to the town council). Seven children were born of this marriage, six sons and a daughter.[69] One of the sons, Georg Christian (baptised in Halle on 7 January 1675, died at Weissenfels before 1720) also practised in Weissenfels as a surgeon, and his son Christian Gottlieb Händel, born at Weissenfels on 9 January 1714, was the person named in Handel's will in 1750. He was at that time an oboist in Copenhagen, so he was one other person from Handel's circle of relatives who had become a professional musician. In the first codicil to his will (August 1756) Handel increased the legacy to Christian Gottlieb, who however must have died soon afterwards.[70] In consequence of this, his two unmarried sisters were substituted as heirs in the third codicil: Christiane Susanne (born at Weissenfels, 17 June 1700), then living in Goslar (Harz / Lower Saxony), and Rahel Sophia (born at Weissenfels, 6 November 1703) living in Pless, Silesia (today the Polish Pszczyna).[71] It is apparent that Handel did not know the name of the younger sister at the time; in naming the elder sister he used the female form of their surname, 'Handelin'.

A second group of bequests relates to the descendants of Handel's sister Dorothea Sophia, who was born in Halle on 6 October 1687 and died at Gut Stichelsdorf (today part of Peissen, north-east of Halle) on 8 August 1718. She was the only one of Handel's natural siblings to have a family: Handel's brother died at birth, and his other sister (Johanna Christiana) died unmarried at the age of 19 in 1709. In 1708 Dorothea Sophia married the jurist Michael Dietrich Michaelsen (born at Bremen, 1681), who in 1726 was promoted to the Royal Prussian war council; he died in Halle on 20 July 1748. There were five children of this marriage (three sons and two daughters) of whom only Johanna Friderica survived to adulthood.[72] The family looked after Handel's mother in Halle, and once Handel had settled in London Michaelsen became his principal contact in Halle concerning family matters. Handel's surviving correspondence is not extensive, but a quarter of the known letters were written to him, over a span of seventeen years: in February 1719 (from London, concerning the delaying of his journey to Germany and the death of his sister), June 1725 (from London), March 1729 (from Venice, announcing his visit to Halle in July), February 1731 (from London, thanking him for looking after his deceased mother), July 1731 (from London, thanking him for dealing with the funeral arrangements for his mother), August 1733 (from London, on the administration of the house in Halle, and anticipating a visit to Halle which did not take place), and August 1736 (from London, about gifts he was sending for the wedding of his niece Johanna Friderica). Two of these letters (August 1731, and 1733) are in German, the others in French; any answering letters have unfortunately not survived.

The daughter Johanna Friderica Michaelsen (born and died in Halle, 20 November 1711 - 24 February 1771), Handel's niece, was married on 6 December 1731 in Halle to Johann Ernst Flörcke (1695-1762); they lived first in Jena, then in Gotha from 1733 to 1755 (that is, including the time that Handel made his will), and finally in Halle, where her husband was Professor of Law. Handel was listed as godfather at her christening in the Marienkirche on 23 November 1711 ('Herr George Friedrich Händel, churfl. [= churfürstlicher] hannoverscher Hoff-CapellMeister').[73] He may have travelled from Hanover to Halle expressly for this event. 'Johanna Friderica Flöerken' (the female form of her surname, and Handel's spelling) became Handel's principal beneficiary, receiving the fruits of his substantial investments in the City of London. She was also originally named as the sole executor of the will, but in the first codicil Handel sensibly added a London co-executor, George Amyand.

The other family members referred to in Handel's will, 'my Cousin Magister Christian August Rotth of Halle in Saxony' and 'my Cousin the Widow of George

---

68 [John Mainwaring], *Memoirs of the Life of the late George Frederic Handel* (London, 1760), pp. 2-4, 8-9.

69 Carl's wife died at Weissenfels in October 1699, and he re-married the following year.

70 The precise date of his death has still to be established, but Handel cannot have known of it when he added the second codicil to his will in March 1757.

71 Handel identifies the place as 'Pless near Teschen': the latter is today the twin town Cieszyn / Český Tesin on the Polish-Czech border. In the German transcript of the third codicil, Handel's bequests of 'Three hundred pounds' are transcribed as '300 £ Sterling'.

72 After the death of Dorothea Sophia, Michaelsen married again, to Christine Sophia Dreissig, and then after her death in 1725 for a third time, to her elder sister Sophia Elisabeth Dreissig.

73 Text as in the baptismal register of the Marienkirche.

Taust, Pastor of Giebichenstein near Halle in Saxony' involve more complex and indirect relationships. Handel's description 'cousin' was probably related to the use of the German term 'Vetter', which originally meant 'father's brother' but in the course of time acquired the meaning of 'mother's brother', and later came to refer to all male relatives, like its French counterpart 'cousin'. Handel obviously used the word in its most general sense in his will; today the meaning is more restricted in German usage and indicates only the son of an uncle or aunt, while 'cousine' is used for a female relative. In the German translation of the third codicil of the will 'Vetter' was used as the equivalent for 'cousin'.[74]

To trace the connection with Christian August Rotth we have to go back a generation, to Handel's maternal aunt, Anna Taust (1654-1725). She was one of the three godparents at Handel's baptism,[75] and in September 1689 she married Christoph Andreas Rotth, a parish priest first in Friedersdorf near Storkow in Brandenburg, and then from 1693 in Grosskugel near Halle, where he died in 1720.[76] Christian August Rotth, Handel's legatee, was the son of Christoph Andreas's brother, Albrecht Christian Rotth (1651-1701), a schoolmaster and Archdeacon at St Ulrich's church in Halle, then from 1692 Preacher at St Thomas's in Leipzig. In spite of Handel's description of him as 'cousin', Rotth was therefore not a direct blood relation of the composer. However, they were both born in 1685, and would probably have been friends from their earliest years, laying the foundation for a close personal friendship. Rotth remained in Halle, and was a Deacon at the St Moritz church from 1713 onwards.[77] In Handel's letter of 20 February 1719 he asked his brother-in-law Michaelsen to pass on greetings 'à Mr. Rotth et a tous les bons Amis', and on the death of Handel's mother in 1730 Rotth sent his printed rhyming verses *Trauer-Zeilen aus Halle in Sachsen nach Engelland* ('Sad lines from Halle in Saxony to England') to his 'much-honoured cousin' ('Hochgeehrten Herrn Vetter'), who he refers to as 'his friend'.[78] In the poem he relates that Handel, when visiting Halle the previous year, had called on him unexpectedly. He was also responsible for another printed poem, 'The lively choir of the Muses', composed for Handel's sixty-fifth birthday in 1750 'in truest friendship', which he evidently sent to London.[79] The spiritual affinity so displayed seems among other things to have been based on a common educational experience. Both of their fathers (Georg Händel and Albrecht Christian Rotth) were probably devotees of orthodox Lutheranism, which had to assert itself against the growing Pietism even in the schools: consequently, the sons may not have been pupils in Halle's Lutheran grammar school, but instead the fathers chose to use private tutors for their upbringing and education.[80] The strong and long-standing personal relationship probably explains why the bequests favoured Christian August Rotth rather than Handel's actual cousins, the children of the marriage of Christian Andreas Rotth and Anna Taust, who were possibly still living. Rotth died in Halle on 5 December 1752, leaving a widow (Maria Sophia, née Limmer, daughter of the head of the Jury Bench in Halle) and two children, so in the first codicil to the will Handel transferred the bequest to the widow, with alternative provision for the children in case she died before him. The names of the widow and children are not given in the codicil.

If Rotth's family relationship to Handel was rather distant, the situation was otherwise with 'the Widow of George Taust', who was connected to him through two separate routes in the family tree. The youngest child of Georg Händel by his first marriage was Handel's step-sister Sophia Rosina (1652-1728). She was the longest surviving member from Handel's generation of the family, dying at the age of 66, beaten only by Handel himself (74). In 1668 she married Philipp Pfersdorff (1619-97), the administrator in Langendorf and Wiedebach, south of Weissenfels, and another of the godparents named at Handel's baptism.[81] In 1686 their daughter Dorothea Elisabeth (born in Langendorf, 13 March 1673) married Georg Taust (born at Giebichenstein, 19 July 1658, and died there on 11 July 1720), the youngest brother of Handel's mother,

---

74 Handel addressed Johann Gottfried Taust as 'Vetter' in his letter of 22 June 1750 (see Marx, 'Ein unveröffentlichter Brief'), and as it happens this was correct in the stricter sense, through one of the paths of their family relationship.

75 The entry in the register (translated) describes her as 'the spinster Anna, daughter of Herr Georg Taust, deceased, former parish priest of Giebichenstein'. The other godparents were Philipp Pfersdorff (see note 80, below) and Zacharias Kleinhempel ('Amts Barbier auffm Näumarckt alhier'), the husband of Georg Händel's eldest daughter by his first wife.

76 Grosskugel is to the southeast of Halle and has been part of the parish of Kabelsketal since 2004.

77 The title 'Magister' in Handel's will refers to Rotth's Master's degree from the University of Halle.

78 The text of Rotth's verses is printed in *Händel-Handbuch* iv: *Dokumente zu Leben und Schriften* (Leipzig, 1985), pp. 183-4, and (with an English précis) in Deutsch, *Handel*, pp. 856-9.

79 *Händel-Handbuch* iv, p. 434; Deutsch, *Handel*, p. 680. Only the title-page of the poem has survived.

80 See Lieselotte Bense, 'Neue Erkenntnisse zu den verwandtschaftlichen Zusammenhängen zwischen den Familien Taust, Rotth und Händel', in *Genealogie. Deutsche Zeitschrift für Familienkunde* 43 (1993), Heft 11/12, pp. 705-19.

81 The baptismal register in the Marienkirche identifies him as 'Herr Philipp Fehrsdorff, hochfl.[= hochfürstlich] Sächs[ischer] Verwalter Zu Langendorff'. For the Pfersdorff family, see Bernd Hofestädt and Lieselotte Bense, 'Von Händelschen Familiensinn', in Bernd Hofestädt (ed.), *Die Familie Händel und Halle* (Ekkehard. Neue Folge xiii, Halle 2006), pp. 48-59.

Allegorical study for a memorial print by G.B. Cipriani, showing Handel and music from Messiah

who had succeeded his father as Pastor of Giebichenstein. Because of the wide spread in the age-groups as a result of the two marriages of Handel's father, there was therefore an unusual situation: the daughter of Handel's half-sister (on his father's side of the family) married his uncle (on his mother's side). In addition to naming Dorothea herself for a bequest, Handel also remembered her children.

There were eight children of the marriage and, according to the information that Handel had when he wrote his will, six of these were alive in 1750. He had to amend the provisions of the will in the first codicil (August 1756) because Dorothea herself had died in the meantime (at Giebichenstein, on 17 December 1752), and so had another of her children.[82] By the time Handel himself died, the number had reduced further, to four. There was a dispute with the English executor of Handel's will as to the terms of the administration in this situation: whether the bequest from the first codicil (£1,500: five children with £300 each) should be divided among the four remaining children, or whether the sum should be £1,200 (four children with £300 each). The four surviving children who became beneficiaries were: Christiana Dorothea Taust (born at Giebichenstein, 8 September 1696); Johann Georg Taust (born at Giebichenstein, 25 March 1691, died at Neumarkt, 5 February 1764, Deacon at St Laurentius church, Neumarkt); Johann Gottfried Taust (born at Giebichenstein, 5 August 1698, buried in Halle, 7 November 1780, schoolmaster at the Lutheran grammar school in Halle); and Johann Friedrich Taust (born at Giebichenstein, 13 June 1706, died at Artern in 1791, clerk in a saltworks in Artern).

Handel had probably kept up his contacts with Dorothea Elisabeth Taust especially on account of her connections with his mother's origins in Giebichenstein, but was not so close to the children of Sophia Rosina's other daughter Maria Sophia Pfersdorff (1678-1719), who in 1691 had married Caspar Mangold (d. 1725), the steward in Langendorf for the court of Sachsen-Weissenfels, and later Bürgermeister in Weissenfels. Of their children, Georg Caspar Mangold (1693-1749) was a professional musician (he was from 1722 to 1746 a cellist in the Weissenfels Hofkapelle), and so was his son of the same name (identified as court organist in Weissenfels for a period from 1741 onwards), who might still have been alive in 1750. Similarly he may have lost touch with Sophia Rosina's son, Johann Christian Pfersdorff (1681-1762), the head forester in Pirmasens,[83] who was certainly still alive in 1750. Furthermore, there is no mention in Handel's will of the children of Handel's half-sister Anna Barbara (married name Metzel, d. 1680), nor of those of his half-sister Dorothea Elisabeth (married names Beyer [widowed], then Kleinhempel). This may have been because in 1750 none of their children were still alive, or because Handel had had no further communication with them.

Of the four named relatives in 1750 who were to receive shares of the inheritance, only Johanna Flörcke, the principal beneficiary, was still alive in 1759; the others were represented now by their widow, sisters or children. On 25 April 1759 the *Hollsteinischer unpartheyische Correspondent* reported Handel's death with the comment: 'He has left a legacy of 2000 pounds sterling to his relatives in Germany'.[84] That is clearly not correct, and the understatement could have been intended to discourage possible claims from other relatives. In fact, on 11 October 1759 the sum of £9000 was transferred through George Amyand from Handel's Annuities account with the Bank of England to 'Johanna Friderica Floerken. Wife of Johan Ernst Floerken, Director of the University in Halle in Saxony'.[85] But the pleasure over that must have been short-lived. Her husband, from 1755 Ordinarius of the Faculty of Jurisprudence in the University of Halle, and from 1757 Director of the University, was in 1762 taken as a hostage for the city of Halle in connection with the Seven Years' War (1756-63) and brought to Nuremberg, where he died later the same year, on 9 June. Nine years later, in 1771, she also was buried.

82 One of those who had died must have been Johann Christian Taust (born at Giebichenstein, 16 May 1693), who had studied law in Halle.
83 Pirmasens, today in Rheinland-Pfalz, belonged in Handel's time to the Landgrave territory of Hesse-Darmstadt.
84 *Händel-Handbuch*, iv, p. 533.
85 Deutsch, *Handel*, p. 838; *Händel-Handbuch*, iv p. 550.

AN EXCEPTIONAL ESTATE

RICHARD CREWDSON

H ANDEL DIED A RICH MAN. Of the composers who have made careers in the London theatres during modern times, Andrew Lloyd Webber probably provides the closest comparison in terms of the accumulation of substantial wealth, driven by a strong sense of purpose. Both composers took the plunge to promote and produce their own works. They personally accepted the risk of failure and, so long as the production was profitable, the profit, in whole or part, belonged to them; the financial benefit which accrued to them through repeated performances amounted to a great deal more than could be realised from one-off performances in a concert hall. Both also saw financial benefits from the popularity of their music among a wider public beyond that of the London theatres, through income from the publication of their works.[86] In Handel's case, his theatre earnings were supported by a substantial income from court pensions.

However, the growth in Handel's personal fortune was by no means a steady or continuous one.[87] Despite his enviable reputation, anxious periods occurred once he decided to cut the traces and become his own master, from 1729 onwards, in the presentation of operas and oratorios. During the 1730s he had to face formidable competition, health problems and the fickle taste of his London patrons. For four years (1739-1743) he had no money or investments at the Bank of England.[88] But during the last twelve years of his life Handel's fortune grew, presumably supported by the profits arising from each successive oratorio season, when he successfully abandoned the subscription system and created a free market in tickets for his performances. Although it has proved impossible to establish an exact valuation of his estate at his death, there can be no doubt that the figure put upon it by James Harris of 'near £20,000' was a close approximation.[89] £20,000 in current terms today would have bought Handel an expensive motor car or a long cruise, but given the vast change in the purchasing power of the pound over the last 250 years, what does that sum really represent in twenty-first-century currency, and how did it compare, in terms of today's money, with the estates of Handel's contemporaries in the world of London music and theatre?

An authoritative estimate of the relative value of the pound in the year 1750 can be found in a House of Commons Library Research Paper published in 2006, entitled 'Inflation: the Value of the Pound 1750-2005'.[90] The authors concluded that in 1750 a 'decimal penny' (a notional unit of currency, as there were actually 240 pennies in the pound until the change to decimal currency in 1971) would be valued at more than £1 in 2005, and that the actual differential was nearly 150. This is of course a simple and crude currency equation, taking no account of changes in the relative values of goods and services over a period of 250 years.[91] Nevertheless Handel's estate, if valued today on that basis, would therefore be worth £3 million or thereabouts, and would have been vastly increased to a figure rivalling the Lloyd Webber fortune if any form of mechanical reproduction rights or a proper system for the collection of performance fees had then been in existence. But even without this increment the many beneficiaries under Handel's 1750 will, taken in conjunction with his four subsequent codicils, were generously treated and, having satisfied them all (including a legacy of £1,000, or £150,000 in today's values, to the 'Society for the Support of Decayed Musicians and their Families'), the residuary bequest which he left to his niece

[86] Modern income from performing rights was not available to Handel, but in addition to payments from publishers he may have received some income from the supply of manuscript copies to connoisseurs.
[87] For a detailed analysis of Handel's capital funds from his earliest days in London until his death, see Harris, 'Handel the Investor'.
[88] Harris, op. cit., p. 542. See, however, the statement by Charles Jennens in a letter of October 1738 that Handel was currently 'overstocked with money' (Deutsch, *Handel*, p. 466).
[89] Letter of James Harris, 28 April 1759, in Burrows and Dunhill, *Music and Theatre*, p. 339.
[90] House of Commons Library, Research Paper 06/09.
[91] See Robert D. Hume, 'The economics of culture in London, 1660-1740', *Huntington Library Quarterly*, 69/4 (2006), pp. 487-553, esp. pp. 490-2.

Handel monument in Vauxhall Gardens. Engraving, ca.1790

Johanna Friderica Floercke amounted to what would be the equivalent of £1.3 million today.[92]

Comparisons are usually 'odious', and those between rich and poor are often the most heart-rending. One feels great sympathy for the many musicians, with their many different hard-luck stories, who appealed for help from the Fund for Decayed Musicians: most of them were too poor even to consider making a will. Nevertheless, Handel's achievements and perseverance in the face of misfortune, illness and at times hostility, thereby creating a great estate for himself from humble beginnings, demand sincere respect. If he had not possessed that streak of entrepreneurial determination and courage he too might have been numbered amongst those asking for assistance.

For most eighteenth-century English composers a distinguished career and a high reputation were no guarantee of ongoing wealth, especially if they were fortunate (or unfortunate) enough to enjoy a long life. John Christopher Pepusch who died aged 85 in 1752 had, like Handel, enjoyed the patronage of the Duke of Chandos, had collaborated in the very successful production of *The Beggar's Opera* and had pioneered secular musical education for boys at the reorganised Academy of Ancient Music. He too was a founder member of the Society of Musicians and contributed to its funds in 1742 and 1744. He was elected Fellow of the Royal Society in 1746. In middle life he had enjoyed years of prosperity, having married the celebrated soprano Margherita de l'Epine in 1718, but unfortunately that was only a year before her retirement from the stage, when her very substantial earnings ceased. By the time she died in 1746 not much could have been left and, although no details of the size of his estate survive, the terms of his will suggest that at his death his assets were few, and his cash resources very meagre. He left three legacies of five guineas, one of three guineas and one of two guineas. Two other specific bequests, his gold medal presented by the Academy of Music and his gold snuff-box, appear to have been his other principal assets. In his later years he lived in the Charterhouse, where he was organist, and apparently possessed no real estate of his own. He had, however, accumulated riches of another sort in an extensive library of music associated with his antiquarian interests, including the volume now known as the Fitzwilliam Virginal Book.

Handel was a wealthy bachelor, with no immediate family commitments in London. Women played a small part in his life and constituted no drain on his purse. As singers, they were contracted as required for performances; as domestics, he had a housekeeper and other servants, who by his will were well rewarded for their services. The bequests to Mrs Palmer, Mrs Mayne and Mrs Donnellan in the last codicil to Handel's will probably reflect some social attachments, and according to Charles Burney Handel 'was very fond of Mrs Cibber, whose voice and manners had softened his severity for her want of musical knowledge'.[93] The singer Susanna Cibber was the sister of Thomas Arne, whose personal and professional life was much more troubled than Handel's, 'meeting with disappointments, half successes or downright failure',[94] and whose experiences with the opposite sex were, one might say, rather more typical than Handel's. Having had singing lessons from her brother as a child, Susanna was a regular performer in Arne's earlier works, and came in and out of his life. His wife Cecilia was also a singer and they worked together for about twelve years before the marriage broke up.[95] Despite successes in the 1760s (*Artaxerxes, Love in a Village* and the masque *The Arcadian Nuptials*) Arne was in financial difficulties by 1770 and was being threatened with litigation by his wife for failure to maintain her. Seven years later they were reconciled, apparently through the tears of his little great niece, but only a few months later he died.[96] He left all his estate jointly to 'my beloved wife Cecilia' and to his son Michael, but not before he had recorded for posterity his unforgiving hostility to certain unnamed persons, presumably in his employment: 'I give and bequeath [to Cecilia and Michael] the sad remains of my once excellent Organ strangled trod to pieces and ruined by and through the villainy of wicked servants'. His wife and son were to

---

92 Handel's bequest provided 'by far the largest benefaction' to the Fund administered by the Society: see Pippa Drummond, 'The Royal Society of Musicians in the Eighteenth Century', *Music & Letters*, 59/3 (1978), p. 279.
93 Charles Burney, *Commemoration*, 'Sketch', p. 35.
94 C. L. Cudworth, 'Boyce and Arne: the "Generation of 1710"', *Music & Letters*, 41/2 (1960), p. 136.
95 As Cecilia Young, Arne's wife had sung for Handel before her marriage.
96 Hubert Langley, *Dr Arne* (Cambridge, 1938), p. 61.

'dispose of the same to the best advantage and share the profits equally between them'.

There are very few references to money sums in Arne's will. His wife and son would have to make what they could financially from exploiting his works, which were to be 'called forth used and employ'd for the mutual benefit profit and emolument of my said son as well as wife'. Then there is a proviso. Arne naturally foresaw that Michael would be the entrepreneur, so Cecilia had to have some safeguard against hasty decisions and false accounting: 'for security of which to the said Cecilia she has and shall have … an unquestionable right to be satisfied as to the probability of success in the undertaking and an equal right to elect a trustee or treasurer to sit in the Treasurer's Office on all and every night [of performance]'. The same arrangements were to apply 'if either of my said dramatic productions shall by their mutual consent be disposed of to their mutual profit or advantage to either of the Patent Theatres [i.e. Covent Garden and Drury Lane]'.

Thomas Arne had been a pupil of Maurice Greene's great friend Michael Festing.[97] Greene's daughter Katherine married Festing's elder son, another Michael. The social status of the Greene family was rather grander than those of Maurice's contemporaries. His grandfather had been Recorder (Chief Magistrate) of London; his father was a Royal Chaplain and a Canon of Salisbury. In his will he describes himself as 'Maurice Greene of Bois Hall in the Parish of Navestock', and at the date of his death in 1755 he was the owner of two substantial farms in Navestock, Essex, although he had inherited this property from a 'cousin' (actually his uncle's bastard son) late in life. In the end he was therefore a man of independent means, and could be confident of passing on an estate which would ensure that his wife Mary (a cousin of Jeremiah Clarke) and his daughter Katherine Festing (the only survivor of five children) were comfortably provided for, regardless of any value that might be attached to his music. The latter amounted to very little, as he had effectively reduced the value of his own compositions to zero by bequeathing his music to William Boyce, 'he having promised not to publish any of my Works'. In his last years Greene had been assembling a great collection of church music with the intention of publishing it and sending copies to every English cathedral.[98] He bequeathed the whole collection to William Boyce together with 'all my books relating to that science'.

The two farms in Navestock had a yearly rental value of £132 (£20,000 in today's values) and £50 (£7,500) respectively. As virtually all the estate remained in the family it was not valued in the will, but Trustees were appointed to sell the residue and reinvest in government securities. Each of the Trustees received a legacy of £100 but there was also one very substantial pecuniary legacy. By the combined effect of the will and a codicil Dr Greene gave the sum of £1,000 (£150,000) to Dorothy Prince, spinster, 'in consideration of her family behaviour to my family'. Researches have failed to reveal who this lady was and what her services to the family had been, but the size of the sum involved (equal to Handel's bequest to the Fund for Decayed Musicians) is remarkable.

So far we have observed one composer who died with a very modest estate, one through whose hands much money had passed and little remained, and one who was cushioned by his circumstances.[99] The only English composer of that generation who could be said to have enjoyed a successful and prosperous career entirely by his own efforts was William Boyce, who began life as the son of a Beadle of a City Livery Company and was a chorister at St Paul's Cathedral; at his death he was entombed beneath the dome of the cathedral, although he had not held office as organist there. He was renowned for his equable temperament. The two great English music historians of the eighteenth century, Charles Burney and John Hawkins, remembered him as follows: 'there was no professor [i.e. professional musician] whom I was ever acquainted with, that I loved, honoured, & respected more', and 'he … was mild and gentle in his deportment, above all resentment against such as envied his reputation'.[100] This is not the image that one would normally associate with a great composer, and despite his

---

97 Although Michael Festing, a violinist, was not wealthy, his brother John, a flautist, left a considerable estate, with bequests of £2,000 and £1,000 to his children, and Bank Stock of £7,000.
98 See H. Diack Johnstone, 'The genesis of Boyce's *Cathedral Music*', *Music & Letters*, 56/1 (1975), pp. 26-40.
99 Other leading London musicians acquired wealth, including real estate, as a result of advantageous marriages (John Stanley, Charles King) or family inheritance (Samuel Wesley).
100 Letter from Burney to John Wall Callcott, 14 November 1803, relating to a reference for Boyce's son (Osborn Collection, Yale University); J[ohn] H[awkins], 'Memoirs of Dr. William Boyce' as a Preface to the second edition of Boyce's *Cathedral Music* (3 vols, London, 1788), i, p. xi.

appointment as Master of the King's Music, in succession to Greene, there is nothing to suggest that Boyce derived much wealth from his compositions, or from sales of his great 3-volume collection of *Cathedral Music,* based on the material that Maurice Greene had bequeathed to him, and which was published between 1760 and 1773.[101] Nevertheless his estate included £500 in 4% Consolidated Annuities (£60,000 equivalent, assuming a 20% discount in the value of the stock), so Boyce died reasonably well off, although he does not appear to have owned any real estate.[102]

One need look no further for confirmation that no other English composer of the eighteenth century, as a result of his professional activity, attained the dizzy heights of wealth enjoyed by Handel. It was of course Handel as impresario, not as composer, who scaled the cliff and guarded his crock of gold. Our comparative analysis should therefore be directed away from the musicians and towards the theatre managers, in order to see where comparable accumulation of wealth was to be found. Two obvious exemplars offer themselves for consideration: John Rich, manager of the Covent Garden theatre, and the fabulously wealthy David Garrick.

The Theatre Royal, Covent Garden, was the principal venue for Handel's oratorio seasons from 1743 onwards;[103] Handel had his 'Great Organ' installed there, and in August 1757 he bequeathed the organ to Rich in the third codicil to his will. John Rich's own will, dated 21 May 1761, plainly sets out what Rich regarded as his own principal asset:

> Whereas I am intitled to and possessed of the Theatre Royal in Covent Garden and the Grounds Estates and all other the furniture thereof or thereunto belonging and am also possessed of interested in or intitled unto two several Letters Patent granted by King Charles the Second the One unto Sir William Davenant his Heirs and Executors Administrators and Assigns and the other unto Thomas Killigrew Esquire his Heirs Executors Administrators and Assigns ... by Virtue of which Letters Patent or one of them[104] the said Theatre Royal Covent Garden was erected by me and entertainments of the Stage have been and still continue to be exhibited therein under my Management and Direction and for my sole profit after deducting thereout such charges and expenses as the same are subject and liable to[.]

Anticipating that his son-in-law John Beard, who was one of his executors, might wish to continue the management of the theatre, Rich included detailed instructions in his will as to the financial basis on which the management could be carried on in such a way that his widow's interest in the property was fully protected. The manager's salary was not in any circumstances to exceed £300 (£45,000) per annum. Beard was evidently not only a great tenor, who created many of Handel's roles, but also a good man of business. When he finally sold the theatre in 1767, the price he obtained was £67,000 (about £10 million in current terms).

John Rich had made his stage reputation as the pantomime character Harlequin, using the stage name 'Lun'. David Garrick's reputation as an actor stood far above this, although he too started in pantomime, but again it was as an impresario that he achieved his massive fortune. Rich had Covent Garden; Garrick (having purchased a renewal of the licence in 1747) had Drury Lane, which he used for opera as well as plays and pantomimes.[105] In his will Garrick described his real estate as 'my dwelling house at Hampton and the Outhouses Stables Yards Gardens Orchards Lands and Grounds' together with the 'two islands or Ayots' on the River Thames; also his house in the Adelphi (no doubt overlooking the river). He was also Lord of the Manor of Hendon and, it would appear from the will, of other manors as well. His widow Eva, who had been prima ballerina in an opera troupe directed by Gluck, was to receive an immediate payment after his death of £1,000, a further £5,000 twelve months later, and thereafter an annuity of £1,500 for life. Legacies to other relatives, not including real estate, amounted to £40,000. The total value of these gifts in current terms, again excluding

---

[101] The subscription list for *Cathedral Music* was disappointingly small, and Boyce 'did but little more than reimburse himself the cost of first publication': Johnstone, 'The genesis', p. 32.

[102] The Annuities relating to his estate are recorded in Society of Genealogists, Bank of England Wills: Book 30, Register No. 4882.

[103] Handel gave just one season (1744–5) at the King's Theatre, Haymarket; the only other relevant venue was the Foundling Hospital Chapel, for the annual performances of *Messiah* from 1750 onwards.

[104] The words 'or one of them' appear because Rich was owner of both of the theatre patents that had been created in the 1660s. Rich and his successors in title (until 1834) were actually the only holders of a perpetual patent; performances at Drury Lane during the eighteenth century took place under licences, which were granted either for the life of the holder or for 21-year terms. See Robert D. Hume, 'Theatre as property in eighteenth-century London', *Journal for Eighteenth Century Studies*, 31/1 (2008), pp. 17–46.

[105] In 1776 Garrick sold his 66% share in Drury Lane for £35,000 (=£5.25 million) to Sheridan and others, rather less advantageously than the sum that John Beard had achieved for Covent Garden.

the real estate, would be about twelve and a half million pounds, or four times the size of Handel's.

To own a theatre, to manage one's own productions, to avoid opera and Italian singers with their crippling costs: these were the ways to make a fortune in the eighteenth century. Handel was able to add the personal touch by entertaining his audiences during the *entractes* of the oratorios as soloist in his organ concertos – this even remained as a star turn in his last years when his blindness meant that he could neither read the music nor see the orchestra. It was a tragic irony that his wealth was accruing exponentially as his sight declined. A final irony was that the music publisher John Walsh, who died in the same year that John Beard sold his theatre, was alleged to have left a fortune twice the size of Handel's.[106] He owned no theatres, and in terms of musical publishing he was 'the most successful pirate in London'.[107] With regard to Handel's music, however, he switched from poacher to respectable gamekeeper during the 1730s, and his position as Handel's regular publisher must have contributed substantially to his wealth.

In complete contrast, [John] Christopher Smith and his son were responsible for preserving and sustaining Handel's musical legacy without so much prospect of financial benefit for themselves. In his will Handel left Smith senior, his long-standing copyist and amanuensis, a legacy of £500 (increased to £2,000 by his first codicil) and his music library, as well as his large harpsichord and house organ. Smith died in January 1763, leaving to his son John Christopher 'All my Musick Books and Peices of Musick whether Manuscript or otherwise which were left to me by the last Will & Testament of my Friend George Frederick Handel deceased And also all my other Musick & Books of Musick both in print & manuscript'.[108] In gratitude for the royal pension that he received following the death in 1772 of the Dowager Princess of Wales (King George III's mother), to whom he had been harpsichord master, Smith junior 'presented to the King the rich legacy which Handel had left him, of all his manuscript music, in score'.[109] Neither of the Smiths left any significant financial estate, but we must be grateful to them for preserving and sustaining Handel's musical legacy.

Terracotta modello for the monument to George Frederick Handel (1685-1759) in Westminster Abbey, c.1760

106 See William C. Smith and Charles Humphries, *A Bibliography of the Musical Works published by the firm of John Walsh during the years 1721-1766* (London, 1968), p. x. At the time of Walsh's death contemporary journals and newspapers put the figure at £30,000 or £20,000.
107 H. Diack Johnstone, 'Greene and the *The Lady's Banquet*: a case of double piracy', *The Musical Times*, 108/1 (January 1967), p. 36.
108 For a transcript of the elder Smith's will, see James S. Hall, 'John Christopher Smith, Handel's friend and secretary', *The Musical Times*, 96/3 (March 1955), pp. 132-4.
109 [Coxe], *Anecdotes*, p. 55. The substance of Coxe's description is probably correct, though the will of Smith senior shows that his son had not received Handel's music directly from the composer.

TRANSLATIONS OF FRENCH TEXTS

Lcm MS 2190 f. 1r, marginal note:

I received this will of my aunt, Auguste Kroll, of the Taust family in Halle. My aunt Madame widow Auguste Kroll had received it with the inheritance of her late uncle Georg Frederic Handel of Halle, who died in London.[110]   Dr. Roehrig.

Lcm MS 2192

Halle, 19 September 1759

Eight days after seeing this, Mr George Amyand Esquire in London, one of the executors of the will of the late Mr George Frederic Handel, is required to pay to the order of Mr Gottlieb Leemann, Banker in Hamburg, the sum of fifteen hundred pounds sterling, which our late above-mentioned cousin Mr Handel desired to bequeath to us by his will of 1 June 1756 [*sic*]. This receipted bill of exchange will serve Mr Amyand as a receipt and discharge that he has entirely satisfied the last will of the testator towards us.

To Mr George Amyand Esquire in London,
one of the executors of the will of the late Mr Handel.

    Jean George Taust
    Jean Geofroy Taust
    Jean Frederyk Taust
    Christiane Dorothea Taust
    Charles Auguste Fritze, trustee for the
    above-mentioned Miss Taust

We, Director of the Community and Assessors of French Royal Justice, certify and attest that in our presence the above-mentioned gentlemen and Miss Taust have had the present bill of exchange written by Mr Jean Frederic Taust, their brother and also an interested party in the legacy of fifteen hundred pounds sterling, and subsequently signed in their own hand by all the legatees and by Mr Fitze the trustee. In witness whereof we have sent the present certificate under the seal of our jurisdiction and the approval of the Director and Judge. Written in Halle in the Duchy of Magdeburg on 19 September 1759.   Jean Adam Michel

Today, 10 October [*space*] in the year of Grace seventeen hundred and fifty-nine, at the request of Messrs Henry and John Shiffner, agents in this city of London, bearers of the bill of exchange a copy of which is written in the accompanying document, I, Benjamin Bonnet, Notary and Royal and Public Scrivener in London, by Royal authority duly admitted and sworn, have shown and displayed the original of this bill of exchange to George Amyand esquire, agent in this aforesaid city, to whom it is addressed, and I have asked him to accept the same; to which he replied that he will not accept the said bill of exchange because it is drawn for the sum of fifteen hundred pounds sterling, whereas it should be drawn for twelve hundred.

For this reason I, the appointed notary for the above request, have protested, as I now protest formally in this document, both against the issuers of this bill of exchange and the other holders in due course, all expenses, damages and interests already suffered and to be suffered because of the refusal to accept the aforesaid bill of exchange. Made and protested in London in the presence of William Wallis and J[ac]ob Smith of the aforesaid city of London as witnesses.

        In testimonium veritatis [*In witness of the truth*]
        Ben: Bonnet, Public Notary
                1759:

---

110 'Uncle' is used here in a general sense, comparable to Handel's use of 'cousin' in his will, to denote an indirect male relative from a previous generation. Auguste Kroll was probably the daughter of Johann Gottfried Taust. Dr Otto Roehrig also formerly owned Handel's letter of 22 June 1750 to Taust: see Marx, 'Ein unveröffentlichter Brief', p. 221.

TRANSLATIONS OF GERMAN TEXTS

Lcm MS 2191, f. 1r

Ich George Friedrich Hændel mach dieses fernere Codicill zu meinem Testament, weil mein Vetter Christian Gottlieb Hændel verstorben, so vermache ich seiner Schwester Christiana Susanna Hændelin zu Goslar 300 £ Sterlings und seiner Schwester, welche sich zu Pleß un weit Teschen in Schlesien aufhält 300 £ Sterlg:

Ich ver mache an John Esqr meine GroßOrgel, welche auf dem Königl: Theatro in Covent Garten stehet.

Ich ver mache an Charles Jennes Esqr: zwey Gemählde, dem alten Manns Kopff, und dem alten Weibs Kopff, gemahlt von Denner.

Ich ver mache an - Granville Esqr: in Holles Street die Landschafft, eine Aussicht des Reihns gemahlt von Rombrand, und eine andere Landschafft, welche von der nehmlichen Hand gemahlt seyn soll, wo mit er mir vor einer geraumen Zeit ein Present gemacht. Ich ver= mache eine saubere Abschrifft der zwantzig und aller übrigen Partien meines Oratorii, genannt der Messias an das Findlings Hospital, in Uhrkund pp dn: 4ten Aug: 1757.   George Friedrich Hændel

an oben geschriebenen Tage und Jahre ist dieses Codicil

gedachten George Friedrich Hændel vor gelesen und
(by him)
von ihm unter zeichnet und publiciret in unserer Gegenwart
Tho J. Harris, John Maxwell.

SPECIFICATIONS OF THE DOCUMENTS

Page sizes Measurements are in cm., to the nearest 0.5 cm. These are necessarily approximate, because the leaves (as manufactured, or as trimmed) rarely have square corners and parallel edges.

Folio conjunctions Conjunct leaves are indicated by '&', as for example '1&4'. The most likely original state is listed. Few of the pages are still joined, and subsequent conservation may have divided leaves or introduced the possibility of 'false gatherings', but the original patterns of conjugate leaves can reasonably be established from the combinations of watermark figures.

Folding patterns All pages of the documents are now fully opened, but have fold marks indicating previous states. Folds are recorded by folios (i.e. ignoring folds for leaf-conjunctions) and are coded here as 'H' (horizontal) and 'V' (vertical). 'H1' and 'V1' indicate single folds, at approximately the half-way point unless otherwise noted. H2^4 indicates two horizontal folds, dividing the page area by four (i.e. pages were folded half-way, and then again); V2^3 indicates two vertical folds (usually folding inwards), dividing the page area into three approximately equal areas. Where a document was subjected to both horizontal and vertical folds, it is usually possible to establish a sequence from the appearance of the fold marks: 'V2^3 + H1' indicates that the vertical folds were made first.

The Coke Copy (Foundling Museum, London, Gerald Coke Handel Collection 5193)

Pages reproduced: all, incorporating also an additional original leaf, designated f. 1a, which is reproduced from photographic copies in the Coke Collection.

Page sizes: f. 1: 22.5 x 18; ff. 2, 3: 30 x 18.5; f.4: 32 x 20.5

Folio conjunctions: 1&1a, 2&3; f. 4 is a separate leaf. The first codicil was written on the first leaf of a bifolium (f. 2), then the empty conjunct leaf was used for the second codicil (f. 3r) and the third codicil (f. 3v).

Folding pattern: f. 1, 1a: V2^3 + H1; ff. 2, 3: H2^4; f. 4 H1 + V1

Folio 1a, originally conjunct with f. 1 in a similar manner to f. 2 in the Probate Copy, was still in place when the will was included in Snoxell's sale (1879), and must have been separated subsequently. It was sold by Stride & Son at Chichester on 3 March 1989 (Lot 371, hammer price £480); the present location and owner are unknown. When the will was folded Handel's inscription ('The Original ...') would have been displayed on one of the outer panels. The leaf, as sold in 1989, was laid on a later sheet with a manuscript annotation at the head of the recto: 'The following piece is in the handwriting of Handel and is his / endorsement on the outer cover of his holograph will which he wrote / out in duplicate'.

Seal: on f. 4v, man's head in profile, on red wax. Illustrated on p.7.

The Probate Copy (The National Archives UK, Kew, PROB 1/14)

Pages reproduced: all pages of the will. The accompanying affidavits (f. 7r, f. 9r) were written on the first pages of bifolia, of which the remaining pages are still empty; the blank pages (ff. 7v, 8, 9v, 10) are not reproduced.

Page sizes: ff. 1, 2: 23 x 18.5; ff. 3, 4: 31 x 19; ff. 5, 6: 32.5 x 20.5; ff. 7, 8: 31.5 x 19.5; ff. 9,10: 31 x 19.5

Folio conjunctions: 1&2, 3&4, 5&6, 7&8, 9&10. The first codicil was written on the first leaf of a bifolium (f. 3), then the empty conjunct leaf was used for the second codicil (f. 4r) and the third codicil (f. 4v). Subsequently ff. 5 & 6 probably acted as a wrapper for the codicils (i.e. enclosing ff. 3 & 4), and possibly the original will (ff. 1 & 2) as well.

Folding pattern: ff. 1–6: V2^3 + H1, subsequently V1; ff. 7–10 probably similar.

Seal: on f. 5v, a similar image to that on the Coke copy, on red wax.

The Executor's Copy (Royal College of Music, London, MSS 2190–2192)

Pages reproduced: MS 2190 ff. 1r, 3v; MS 2191 ff. 1r, 2v; MS 2192 f.1

Page sizes: MS 2190: 31 x 19; MS 2191: 20.5 x 33.5; MS 2192: 31.5 x 20.5

Folio conjunctions: MS 2190: 1&4, 2&3; MS 2191: 1&2; MS 2192: 1&2

Folding pattern: MS 2190: H2^4 + V1; MS 2191: V1 + H1; MS 2192: H2 + V2^3, subsequently V1.

MS 2191 has a distinctly different paper size, and different style of watermark, from MSS 2190 and 2192: the latter were copied in London, but MS 2191 probably in Germany.

Embossed stamps (rose, in circle with 'HONI SOIT QUI MAL Y PENSE', with crown above, alphabet letters and 'VI PENCE' below) at top left of *rectos*, are found as follows:

MS 2190 f. 1: 3 stamps, letters 'K K'; f. 2: 2 stamps, letters 'H H'

MS 2192 f. 1: 2 stamps, letters 'K K'

These record the duty paid for an authorized copy of a probate document. MS 2192 f. 1v also has a piece of paper with the embossed seal (heraldic badge in a circle, presumably the insignia of the relevant court), stuck onto the page to the left of 'Ben: Bonnet'; the annotation '6^s: 9^d' probably relates to a duty payment.

MSS 2190–2192 are made up as separate loose items, but within a cover sheet, probably from the nineteenth century, with an ink annotation on the front: 'George Frederic Handel / The original German Will with copies of the Will and Codicils / Doctor's Commons London 1757 certified by his Grandson [sic] / Dr Roehrig of Halle / very curious document'.

Facsimiles

In the Name of God Amen.

I George Frideric Handel considering the Uncertainty of human Life doe make this my Will in manner following.
viz.

I give and bequeath unto my Servant Peter le Blond, my Clothes and Linnen, and three hundred Pounds Sterl: and to my other Servants a year Wages.

I give and bequeath to Mr Christopher Smith my large Harpsicord, my little House Organ, my Musick Books, and five hundred Pounds Sterl:

Item I give and bequeath to Mr James Hunter ~~................~~ five hundred Pounds Sterl:

I give and bequeath to my Cousin Christian Gottlieb Handel
of Coppenhagen one hundred Pounds Sterl:

Item I give and bequeath to my Cousin Magister Christian
August Roth of Halle in Saxony one hundred Pounds Sterl:

Item I give and bequeath to my Cousin the Widow of
George Taust, Pastor of Giebichenstein near Halle in
Saxony three hundred Pounds Sterl:
and to Her six Children each two hundred Pounds Sterl:

All the next and residue of my Estate in Bank Annuitys
~~Annuitys~~ or of whatsoever kind or Nature,
I give and bequeath unto my Dear Niece
Johanna Friderica Flöerken of Gotha in Saxony
(born Michaelsen in Halle) whom I make my
sole Execut:rix of this my last Will.

In wittness Whereof I have hereunto set my hand
this 1 Day of June 1750

George Frideric Handel

Coke Copy former conjugate leaf folio 1ar [37]

[38] *Coke Copy former conjugate leaf folio 1av*

I George Fredric Handel make this Codicil to my Will.

I give unto my Servant Peter le Blond Two Hundred Pounds additional to the Legacy already given him in my Will.

I give to Mr Christopher Smith Fifteen Hundred Pounds additional to the Legacy already given him in my Will.

I Give to my Cousin Christian Gottlieb Handel of Coppenhagen Two Hundred Pounds additional to the Legacy already given him in my Will.

My Cousin Magister Christian August Roth being dead I Give to his Widow Two Hundred Pounds and if she shall die before me I give the said Two Hundred Pounds to her Children.

The Widow of George Taust and one of her Children being dead I give to her Five Children remaining Three Hundred Pounds apiece instead of the Legacy given to them by my Will.

I Give to Doctor Morell of Turnham Green Two Hundred Pounds.

I Give to Mr Newburgh Hamilton of Old Bond Street who has assisted me in adjusting words for some of my Compositions One Hundred Pounds.

I make George Amyand Esquire of Lawrence Pountney Hill London Merchant Coexecutor with

my Niece mention'd in my Will and I give
him Two Hundred Pounds which I desire him
to accept for the Care and Trouble he shall take
in my Affairs.   In Witness whereof I have
hereunto set my Hand this Sixth day of August
One Thousand Seven Hundred and Fifty Six.

George Frideric Handel

On the day and year above
written this Codicil was read
over to the said George Frideric
Handel and was by him Sign'd
and Publish'd in our Presence
Tho: Harris
John Hetherington

I George Frideric Handel do make this farther Codicil to my Will.

My old Servant Peter Le Blond being lately dead I give to his Nephew John Duburk the Sum of Five Hundred Pounds.

I give to my Servant Thomas Bramwell the Sum of Thirty Pounds in case He shall be living with me at the time of my Death and not otherways.

In Witness whereof I have hereunto set my hand this Twenty Second day of March one thousand Seven hundred and Fifty Seven.

On the day and year above written
this Codicil was read
over to the said George
Frideric Handel and
was by him Signd and
Publish'd in our Presence
    Tho: Harris.
    John Hetherington

George Frideric Handel

I George Frideric Handel do make this farther Codicil to my Will

My Cousin Christian Gottlieb Handel being dead, I give to his sister Christiana Susanna Handelin at Goslar three hundred pounds, and to his sister living at Pless near Teschen in Silesia three hundred pounds.

I give to John Rich Esquire my Great Organ that stands at the Theatre Royal in Covent Garden.

I give to Charles Jennens Esquire two pictures, the Old Man's head and the Old Woman's head done by Denner.

I give to ——— Granville Esquire of Holles Street the Landskip, a View of the Rhine, done by Rembrand, & another Landskip said to be done by the same hand, which he made me a Present of some time ago.

I give a fair copy of the Score and all the Parts of my Oratorio called The Messiah to the Foundling Hospital.

In witness whereof I have hereunto set my hand this fourth day of August one thousand seven hundred & fifty seven

George Frideric Handel

On this day & year above written this Codicil was read over to the said George Frideric Handel and was by him signed and published in our presence

Tho: Harris
John Maxwell

I George Friderick Handel make this farther Codicil

I give to the Governours or Trustees of the Society for the Support of decayed Musicians and their Families one Thousand pounds to be disposed of in the most beneficiall manner for the objects of that Charity,

I give to George Amyand Esquire one of my Executors Two Hundred pounds aditional to what I have before given him,

I give to Thomas Harris Esquire of Lincolns Inn Fields Three Hundred Pounds.

I give to Mr. John Hetherington of the First Fruits Office in the Middle Temple One Hundred pounds.

I give to Mr. James Smyth of Bond Street Perfumer Five Hundred Pounds.

I give to Mr. Matthew Dubourg Musician One Hundred Pounds.

I give to my Servant Thomas Bramwell Seventy Pounds aditional to what I have before given him,

I give to Benjamin Martyn Esquire of New Bond street Fifty Guineas.

I give to Mr. John Belchier of Sun Court Threadneedle Street Surgeon Fifty Guineas.

I give all my wearing apparel to my servant John Le Bourk.

I give to Mr. John Gowland of New Bond Street Apothecary Fifty Pounds.

I hope to have the permission of the Dean and Chapter of West=minster to be buried in Westminster Abbey in a private manner at the discretion of my Executor Mr. Amyand and I desire that my said Executor may have leave to erect a monument for me there and that any sum not Exceeding Six

Hundred Pounds be expended for that purpose at the discretion of my said Executor.

I give to Mrs Palmer of Chelsea Widow of Mr Palmer formerly of Chappel Street One Hundred Pounds.

I give to my two Maid Servants each one years wages over and above what shall be due to them at the time of my death. I give to Mrs Mayne of Kensington Widow Sister of the late Mr Batt Fifty Guineas.

I give to Mrs Donnalan of Charles Street Berkley Square Fifty Guineas.

I give to Mr Reiche Secretary for the affairs of Hanover Two Hundred Pounds.

In Witness whereof I have hereunto set my hand and Seal this Eleventh day of April 1759.

G F Handel

This Codicil was read over to the
said George Friderick Handel
and by him Signed and Sealed in the
Presence, on the day and Year
above written, of us.
    A. Rudd
    J. Christopher Smith

In the Name of God Amen.

I George Frideric Handel considering the Uncertainty of human Life doe make this my Will in manner following. viz

I give and bequeath unto my Servant Peter le Blond, my Clothes and Linnen, and three hundred Pounds Sterl: and to my other Servants a Year Wages.

I give and bequeath to Mr Christopher Smith my large Harpsicord, my little House Organ, my Musick Books, and five hundred Pounds Sterl:

Item I give and bequeath to Mr James Hunter ~~————————————————~~ five hundred Pounds Sterl:

I give and bequeath to my Cousin Christian Gottlieb Handel of Coppenhagen one hundred Pounds Sterl:

Item I give and bequeath to My Cousin Magister Christian August Roth of Halle in Saxony one hundred Pounds sterl:

Item I give and bequeath to my Cousin the Widow of George Taust, Pastor of Gibichenstein near Halle in Saxony, three hundred Pounds ste and to Her Six Children each twohundred Pounds sterl:

All the next and residue of my Estate in Bank Annuity's 1746. 1st sub. or of whatsoever Kind or Nature, I give and bequeath unto my Dear Niece Johanna Friderica Flörchen of Gotha in Saxony borne Michaelsen in Halle whom I make my sole Exec.r of this my last Will.

In witness whereof I have hereunto set my hand this 1 Day of June 1750

George Frideric Handel

14th April 1759

George Amyand Esqr. the Executor named in the first Codicil was duly sworn to the Truth of this Will and to the several Codicils hereunto annexed Power reserved to Johanna Friederica ~~Before me~~ Flörchen Wife of _____ Flörchen the Executrix named in the Will

Before me

Geo. Harris,
Surrogate

The Testator died this Day and was of the Parish of St. George Hanover Square in the County of Middlesex

Regd. the Affidavits before this Act

Prov'd at London with four Codicills annexed the 26th April 1759 before the Worshipfull George Harris Doctor of Laws Surrogate by the Oath of George Amyand Esqr. the Executor named in the first Codicill to whom Admn. was granted having been first sworn duly to administer power reserved to make the like grant to Johanna Friderica Flörchen (wife of _____ Flörchen) the neice and Executrix named in the Will, when she shall apply for the same.

5

Will &4 (od) Midx
George Frideric Handel Esq.
April 1759

I George Frideric Handel make this Codicil to my Will.

I give unto my Servant Peter le Blond Two Hundred Pounds, additional to the Legacy already given him in my Will.

I give to Mr. Christopher Smith Fifteen Hundred Pounds additional to the Legacy already given him in my Will.

I give to my Cousin Christian Gottlieb Handel of Coppenhagen Two Hundred Pounds additional to the Legacy already given him in my Will.

My Cousin Magister Christian August Rotth being dead, I give to his Widow Two Hundred Pounds, and if she shall die before me, I give the said Two Hundred Pounds to her Children.

The Widow of George Taust and one of her Children being dead I give to her Five remaining Children Three Hundred Pounds apiece instead of the Legacy given to them by my Will.

I give to Doctor Morell of Turnham Green Two Hundred Pounds.

I give to Mr. Newburgh Hamilton of old Bond Street who has assisted me in adjusting words for some of my Compositions One Hundred Pounds.

I make George Amyand Esquire of Lawrence
Pountney Hill London Merchant Coexecutor
with my Niece mention'd in my Will and I give
him Two Hundred Pounds which I desire him
to Accept for the Care and Trouble he shall take
in my affairs. In Witness whereof I have
hereunto set my Hand this Sixth day of August
One Thousand Seven Hundred and Fifty Six.

       George Frideric Handel

On the day and year above written
this Codicil was read over to the
said George Frideric Handel and
was by him Sign'd and Publish'd
in our Presence
     Tho: Harris.
     John Hetherington.

I George Frideric Handel do make this farther Codicil to my Will.

My Old Servant Peter Le Blond being lately dead, I give to his Nephew John Duburk the Sum of Five Hundred Pounds.

I Give to my Servant Thomas Bramwell the Sum of Thirty Pounds in case He shall be living with me at the time of my death and not otherways.

In Witness whereof I have hereunto set my Hand this Twenty Second day of March One thousand seven Hundred and Fifty Seven.

On the day and year above written this Codicil was read over to the said George Frideric Handel, and was by him sign'd and Publish'd in our Presence Tho: Harris.
John Hetherington

George Frideric Handel

I George Frideric Handel do make this further Codicil to my
will

✗ My Cousin Christian Gottlieb Handel being dead, I give to his
Sister Christiana Susanna Handelin at Goslar three hundred
pounds, and to his Sister living at Ploss near Toschen in Silesia
three hundred pounds.

I give to John Rich Esq.r my Great Organ that stands at the
Theatre Royal in Covent Garden.

I give to Charles Jennens Esq.r two pictures, the Old Man's
head, & the Old Woman's head done by Denner.

I give to ——— Granville Esq.r of Holles Street the
Landskip, a view of the Rhine, done by Rembrand, & another
Landskip said to be done by the same hand, which he gave
me a Present of some time ago.

I give a fair Copy of the Score and all the parts of my
Oratorio called The Messiah to the Foundling Hospital.
In witness whereof I have hereunto set my hand this fourth
day of August, One thousand seven hundred & fifty seven.

George Frideric Handel

On the day and year above written
this Codicil was read over to the
said George Frideric Handel,
and was by him signed and
published in our presence
Tho.s Harris
John Maxwell

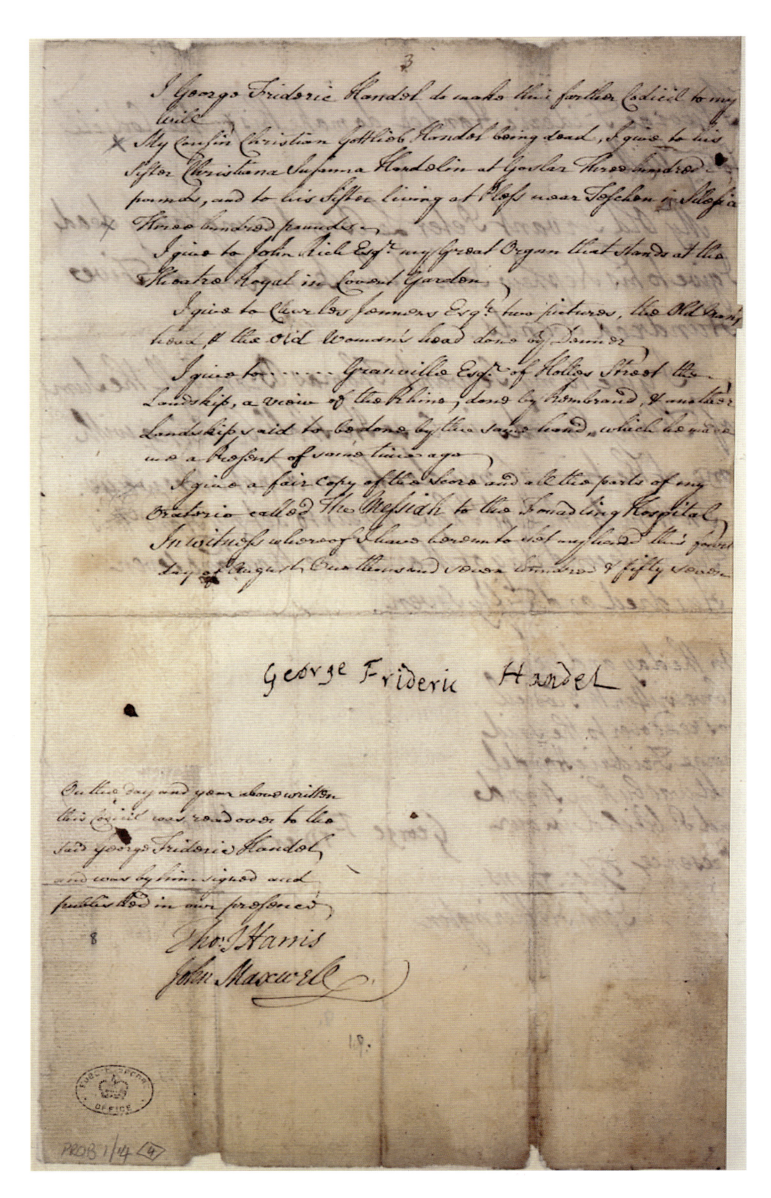

[52] *Probate Copy folio 4v*

I George Friderick Handel make this farther Codicil

I Give to the Governours or Trustees of the Society for the support of decayed Musicians and their Families One Thousand Pounds to be disposed of in the most beneficiall manner for the Objects of that Charity.

I Give to George Amyand Esquire One of my Executors Two Hundred Pounds aditional to what I have before given him.

I Give to Thomas Harris Esquire of Lincolns Inn Fields Three Hundred Pounds.

I Give to Mr. John Hetherington of the First Fruits Office in the Middle Temple One Hundred Pounds.

I Give to Mr. James Smyth of Bond Street Perfumer Five Hundred Pounds.

I Give to Mr. Matthew Dubourg Musician One Hundred Pounds.

I Give to my Servant Thomas Bramwell Seventy Pounds aditional to what I have before given him.

I Give to Benjamin Martyn Esquire of New Bond Street Fifty Guineas.

I Give to Mr. John Belchier of Sun Court Threadneedle Street Surgeon Fifty Guineas.

I Give all my wearing apparel to my Servant John Le Bourk.

I Give to Mr. John Gowland of New Bond Street Apothecary Fifty Pounds.

I hope to have the permission of the Dean and Chapter of Westminster to be buried in Westminster Abbey in a private manner at the discretion of my Executor Mr. Amyand and I desire that my said Executor may have leave to erect a

Monument for me there and that any Sum not Exceeding Six Hundred Pounds be expended for that purpose at the discretion of my said Executor.

I Give to Mrs. Palmer of Chelsea Widow of Mr. Palmer formerly of Chappel Street One Hundred Pounds.

I Give to my two Maid Servants each one years Wages over and above what shall be due to them at the time of my death. I Give to Mrs. Mayne of Kensington Widow Sister of the late Mr. Batt Fifty Guineas.

I Give to Mrs. Donnalan of Charles Street Berkley Square Fifty Guineas.

I Give to Mr. Reiche Secretary for the affairs of Hanover Two Hundred Pounds.

In Witness whereof I have hereunto set my hand and Seal this Eleventh day of April 1759.

G F Hader

This Codicil was read over to the said George Friderick Handel and by him signed and Sealed in the presence, on the day and Year above written of us

A: Rudd
J. Christopher Smith

Probate Copy folio 6r [55]

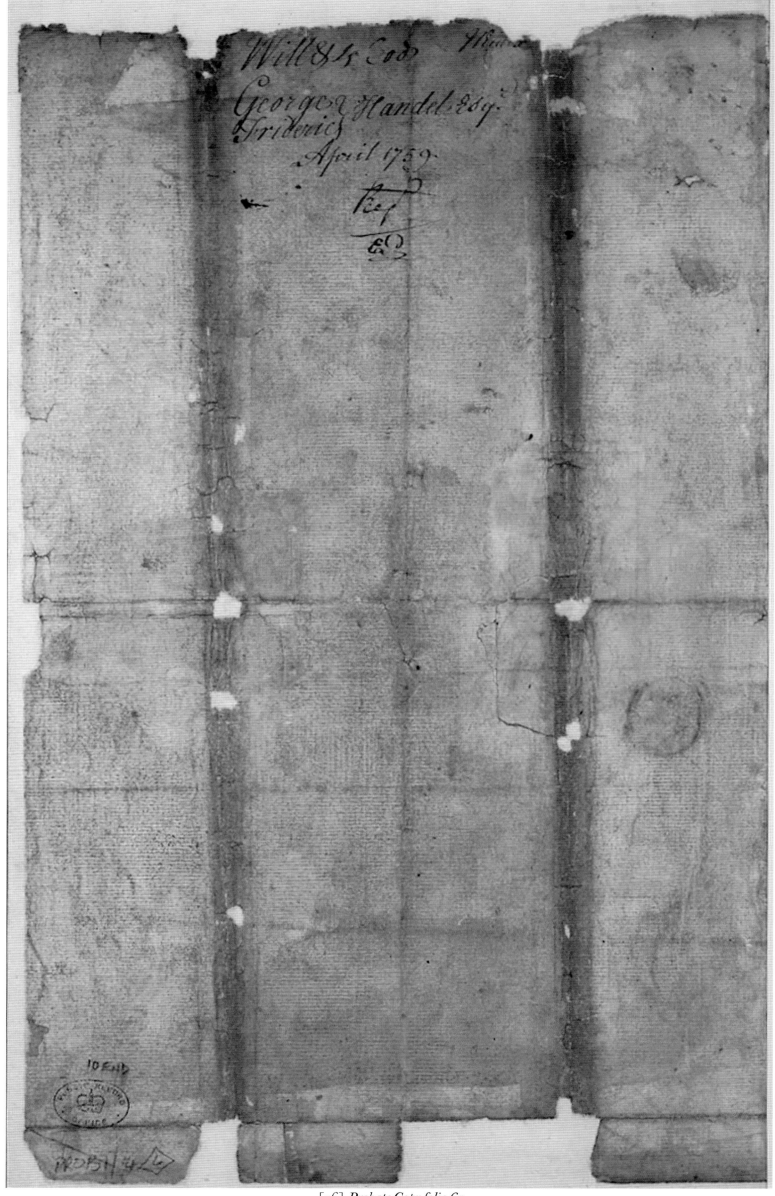

[56] *Probate Copy folio 6v*

23. April 1759

Appeared personally William Brinck of the parish of St. James Westmr. in the County of Middlesex Esqr. and Edward Cavendish of the parish of Paddington in the said County Gentleman and being severally sworn on the Holy Evangelists made Oath Each for himself as follows that they very well knew George Frideric Handel late of the parish of St. George Hanover Square in the County of Middlesex Esqr. deceased and are well acquainted with his Manner and Character of handwriting having often seen him write and they having now carefully viewed the last Will and Testament of the said deceased beginning thus — In the Name of God Amen — and ending thus — In Witness whereof I have hereunto set my hand this 1. Day of June 1750. and thus subscribed. George Frideric Handel. they say that they do verily believe the whole Body and Contents of the said Will and the sd. Name George Frideric Handel thereto subscribed to be all of the proper handwriting of the said George Frideric Handel Esqr. deceased

Same Day
The said William Brinck and Edward
Cavendish were duly sworn

Before me
Arth: Collier
Surro

present Hen: Stevens, N.P.

Wm Brinck
Edwd Cavendish

24.th April 1759

Appeared Personally John Duburk of the Parish of S.t George Hanover Square in the County of Middlesex Gentleman and being sworn on the Holy Evangelists made Oath that he lived with George Frederick Handel Esq.r late of the Parish of S.t George Hanover Square aforesaid died at and for some time next before his Death and was present when a Search was made after his Death for his Will and saith that the last Will and Testament of the said deced hereto annexed dated 1 Day of June 1750 together with the four Codicils thereto respectively dated sixth Day of August 1756 twenty second Day of March 1757 fourth Day of August 1757 and Eleventh Day of April 1759 were all found locked and sealed up together in a Cover in the said deced's Bureau in the deced's late Dwelling House in Brook Street and the said Will at the time it was so found appeared obliterated in the Bequest therein to M.r James Hunter in the very same Manner and Form as it now appears And the Dep.t further says that he well knew the said James Hunter the Legatee and the said James Hunter died in the Life time of the said M.r Handel the Testator

Same Day
The said John Duburk was
sworn to the Truth of this
affid.t Before me

present
John Stevens Not.y Pub.c

John Du Burk

Geo. Harris
Surrogate

Extracted from the Registry of the Prerogative Court of Canterbury.

In the name of God Amen I George Frideric Handel considering the Uncertainty of Human Life do make this my Will in manner following Viz.t I give and bequeath unto my Servant Peter le Blond my Cloths and Linnen and three hundred Pounds Sterl: and to my other Servants a Year's Wages I give and bequeath to Mr: Christopher Smith my large Harpsicord my Little House Organ my Musick Books and five hundred Pounds Sterl: I give and bequeath to Mr: James Hunter five hundred Pounds Sterl. I give and bequeath to my Cousin Christian Gottlieb Handel of Copenhagen One hundred Pounds Sterl. Item I give and bequeath to my Cousin Magister Christian August Rotth of Halle in Saxony One hundred Pounds Sterl. Item I give and bequeath to my Cousin the Widow of George Taust Pastor of Giebichenstein near Halle in Saxony three hundred Pounds Sterl and to her Six Children each two hundred Pounds Sterling. All the rest and residue of my Estate in Bank Annuitys 1746 1.st Sub.n or of whatsoever kind or nature I give and bequeath unto my dear Neice Johanna Friderica Floerchen of Gotha in Saxony (born Michaelsen in Halle) whom I make my Sole Executrix of this my last Will In Witness whereof I have hereunto set my hand this 1.st day of June 1750.

George Frideric Handel

Executor's Copy MS 2190 folio 1r [59]

and Seal this Eleventh day of April 1759 —
G. F. Handel, This Codicil was read
over to the said George Frederic Handel and by
him Signed and Sealed in the presence on
the day and year above written of us,
A. J. Rudd — J Christopher Smith,

Proved at London with four Codicills annexed
the 26th day of April 1759 before the Worshipfull
George Harris Doctor of Laws & Surrogate by the Oath
of George Amyand Esq.r the Executor named in the
~~said Will~~ first Codicil to whom Administration
was granted having been first sworn duly to
administer Power reserved of making the like
grant to Johanna Frederica Floerchen Wife of
Floerchen the Neice and Executrix
named in the Will when she shall apply for
the same, &c.

W.m Legard
Rit. St Eloy
Hen. Stevens.

April 1759.
16

Ich George Friedrich Hændel mache diesen anderen Codicill zu meinem Testament, weil mein Vetter Christian Gottlieb Händel verstorben, so vermache ich seiner Schwester Christiana Susanna Händelin zu Goßlar 300 £ Sterlings und seiner Schwester, welche sich zu Coppenhagen in Pension aufhält 300 £ Ster:

Ich vermache an John Chr myr meine Große Orgel, welche auf dem Königl: Theatro in Covent Garden stehet.

Ich vermache an Charles Jennes Esqr: zwey Gemählde, ihm alten Marcus Kupff, und dem alten Leib Kupff, gemahlet von Denner.

Ich vermache an —— Granville Esqr: in Holles Street die Landschafft, eine Skitze des Rubens gemahlet von Rombrand, und eine andere Landschafft, welche von der nemlichen hand gemahlet seyn soll, wo mit er mir von einiger Zeit ein Præsent gemacht. Ich ver, mache eine saubere Abschrifft der zwanzig und allen übrigen partien meines Oratorii, genannt der Messias an das Findlings Hospital in London, d: 4ten Aug: 1757.
George Friedrich Hændel

an oben geschriebenen tagen und jahren ist dieses Codicil
(by him)
zu dreßen George Friedrich Händel von gelesen und von ihm unter zeichnet und publiciret in unseren Gegenwart
Tho: t: Harris, John Maxwell.

Extract from the Will & Codicills of George Fried: Handel.

Item. I give and beqveath to my Cousin the Widow of George Taust pastor of Gibichenstein near Halle in Saxony three Hundred Pounds Sterling and to her six Childern each Two Hundred Pounds Sterling. Signed 1. Juni 1750.

The Widow of George Taust and one of her Childern being dead I give to her five remaining Childern three hundred pounds a piece instead of the Legacy given to them by my Will. Signed 6. August 1756.

Dr F. L. Roehrig à Halle sur la Saale en Prusse.

2192.

A Halle ce 19.e Septembre 1759

A Huit Jours de Vue il plaira à Monsieur George Amyand Esquire à Londres un des Executeurs Testamentaires de feu le Sieur George Frederic Handel de Payer à l'ordre du Sieur Gottlieb Leemann Banquier à Hambourg la Somme de Quinze Cent Livres Sterlings que feu Nôtre susdit Cousin le Sieur Handel a bien voulu nous leguer par son Testament du 1.° Juin 1756 Cette Lettre de Change acquittée Servira à Monsieur Amyand de Quittance & decharge d'avoir Satisfait entiérement à la dernière Volonté du Testateur à nôtre egard.

A Mr: George Amyand Esquire
Londres un des Executeurs du
Testament de feu le Sieur Handel

                Jean George Faust
                Jean Geofroy Faust
                Jean Frederyk Faust
                Christiane Dorothea Faust
                Charles Auguste Tritze Curateur
                de la dite Demoiselle Faust

Nous Directeur de la Colonie Juge et Assesseurs de la Justice Roiale Francoise en cette Ville Certifions et Attestons qu'en Notre presence les Susdnommés Sieurs et Demoiselle Faust ont fait écrire la presente Lettre de Change par le Sieur Jean Frederic Faust leur frere respectif et aussi Interressé au dit Legs de Quinze Cent Livres Sterlings qu'ensuite tous Legataires ensemble le Sieur Tritze Curateur l'ont Signés de leur propre main Enfoy dequoy nous avons fait expedier le present Certificat sous le Seau de notre Jurisdiction et le Seing du Directeur et Juge Fait à Halle au Duché de Magdebourg le 19.e Septembre 1759

(LS)   Jean Adam Michel

                Aujourdui

Aujourdui dixième d'Octobre   l'an de Grace
Mil sept cent cinquante neuf à la requisition de Mess.rs
Henry & Jean Shiffner Negotiants en cette Ville de Londres,
porteurs de la Lettre de Change dont copie est en l'autre part
ecrite Je Benjamin Bonnet Notaire et Tabellion Royal
& Public à Londres, par Autorité Royalle dûement admis
et Juré, ay montré et exhibé ladite Lettre de Change en
original à George Amyand, Ecuyer, Negotiant en cette
dite Ville, sur qui Elle est tirée, et lui ay demandé
l'acceptation d'Icelle, à quoy il a repondu qu'il n'acceptera
point ladite Lettre de Change parce qu'Elle est tirée
pour la Somme de Quinze Cent livres Sterling, au lieu
qu'elle ne devroit l'être que pour celle de Douze Cent
C'est pourquoy Je dit Notaire à la requete que dessus ay
Protesté comme Je proteste Solemnellement par ces
presentes tant contre les Tireurs de ladite Lettre de
Change que autres qu'il appartiendra du Change rechange
et de tous depens domages et Interests Soufferts et a
Souffrir faute d'acceptation de la d.te Lettre de Change Fait
et protesté à Londres en presence de Guillaume Walles &
Job Smith dud. Londres comme Témoins

In Testimonium Veritatis

Ben. Bonnet   Not. Pub.
1759.

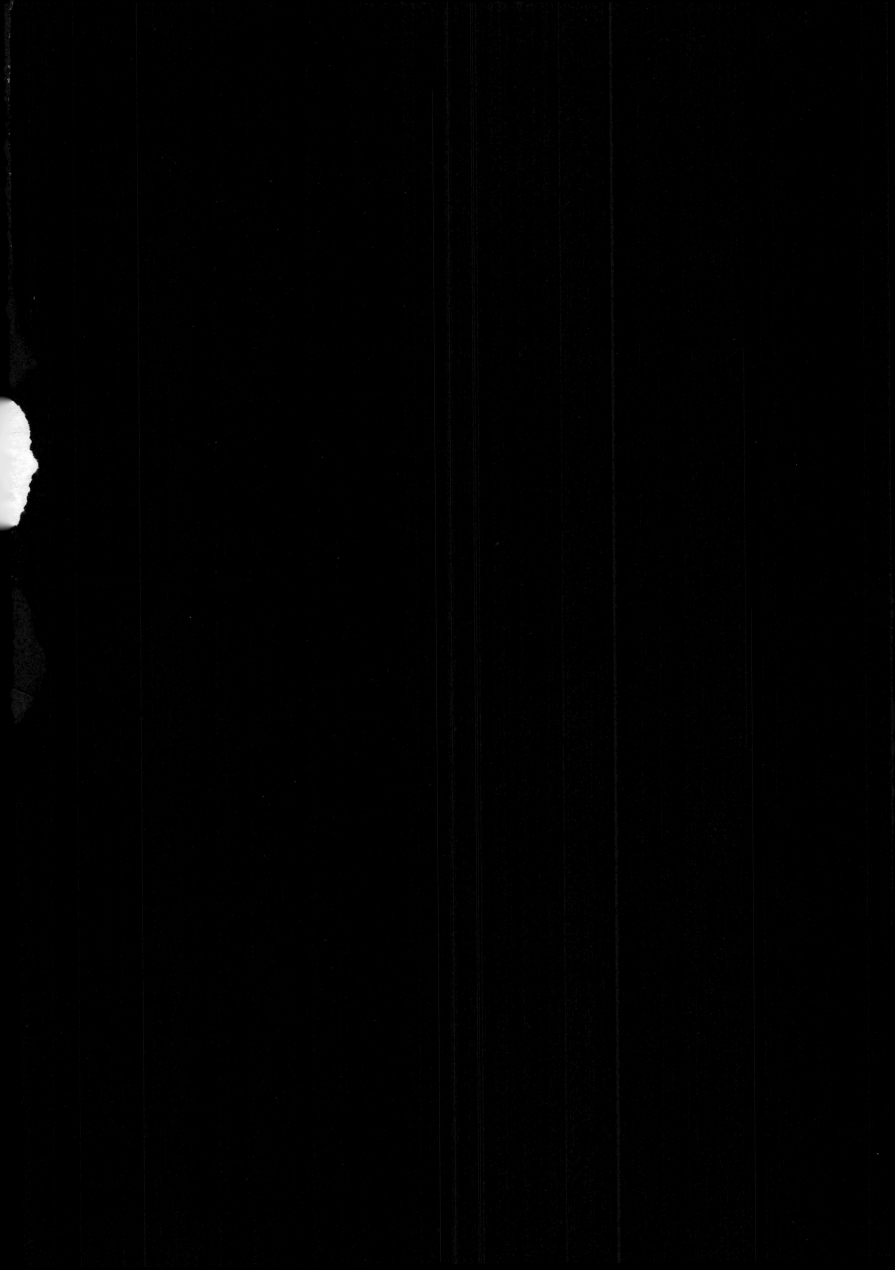